CW01217554

THE
ADMIRAL'S
BOOKSHELF

Praise for *The Sailor's Bookshelf*

"Not only is this unusual book an enjoyable read in itself, but reading all the recommended titles will help counter 'sea blindness' as well as presenting an exciting opportunity to broaden what for many is already a favorite subject."—***Warship***

"This book should be on every sailor's shelf. Admiral Stavridis' love of the sea and love of reading come through on every page."—**Tom Ricks**

"If you are going to read one book this year, you would do well to read *The Sailor's Bookshelf*. The diverse range of topics covered in *The Sailor's Bookshelf* is a key feature in its utility."—***Armchair General***

"This sailor's bookshelf will reward any reader, whether an 'old salt' or a new Sailor straight out of boot camp."—**Master Chief Petty Officer Jim Herdt, USN (Ret.)**

Praise for *The Leader's Bookshelf*

"Admiral Stavridis has shown throughout his career that leaders benefit tremendously from being well read and thinking critically. *The Leader's Bookshelf* is a powerful collection of leadership lessons, drawn from outstanding works of literature, history, and biography. It is an important book from someone I deeply admire."—**Madeleine Albright**

"Unique in its style and structure and outstanding in its personal and confident presentation, *The Leader's Bookshelf* is a singular and valuable contribution to developing effective leaders."—***Naval War College Review***

"I've been trading book recommendations with Admiral Jim Stavridis since we worked together in the Pentagon over a decade ago. He explains better than anyone the power of books to help create leaders, and this is the best possible selection of books to light a path through the most challenging of situations."—**Gen. James Mattis, USMC (Ret.)**

THE ADMIRAL'S BOOKSHELF

ADM. JAMES G. STAVRIDIS, USN (RET.)

NAVAL INSTITUTE PRESS
Annapolis, Maryland

For Captain Bill Harlow
The true professional

Naval Institute Press
291 Wood Road
Annapolis, MD 21402

© 2025 by James G. Stavridis
All rights reserved. No part of this book may be reproduced or utilized in any form or by any means, electronic or mechanical, including photocopying and recording, or by any information storage and retrieval system, without permission in writing from the publisher.

Library of Congress Cataloging-in-Publication Data
Names: Stavridis, James author.
Title: The Admiral's bookshelf / Adm. James Stavridis, USN (Ret.)
Description: Annapolis, Maryland : Naval Institute Press, [2024]
Identifiers: LCCN 2024037351 (print) | LCCN 2024037352 (ebook) | ISBN 9781682472545 (hardback) | ISBN 9781682472569 (ebook)
Subjects: LCSH: Stavridis, James—Books and reading. | Admirals—United States—Biography. | United States. Navy—Biography. | Leadership in literature. | Conduct of life in literature.
Classification: LCC V63.S73 A3 2024 (print) | LCC V63.S73 (ebook) | DDC 028/.8—dc23/eng/20241210
LC record available at https://lccn.loc.gov/2024037351
LC ebook record available at https://lccn.loc.gov/2024037352

♾ Print editions meet the requirements of ANSI/NISO z39.48–1992 (Permanence of Paper).
Printed in the United States of America.

33 32 31 30 29 28 27 26 25   9 8 7 6 5 4 3 2 1
First printing

CONTENTS

Introduction ... 1

1 Never Surrender
   The Old Man and the Sea by Ernest Hemingway ... 8

2 Pick the Right People
   The Godfather by Mario Puzo ... 15

3 Be Your Own Spokesman
   It Worked for Me by Colin Powell ... 23

4 Write with Simplicity and Precision
   The Elements of Style by William Strunk Jr. and E. B. White ... 30

5 Use Humor Often
   A Confederacy of Dunces by John Kennedy Toole ... 40

6 Prepare Deeply for the Key Events
   Crusade in Europe by Dwight David Eisenhower ... 48

7 Stay Physically Fit
   The Boys in the Boat by Daniel Brown ... 57

8	Seek to Innovate *Steve Jobs* by Walter Isaacson	64
9	Work Smart *Flashman* by George MacDonald Fraser	72
10	Think Independently *The Handmaid's Tale* by Margaret Atwood	79
11	Dream without Boundaries *Don Quixote* by Miguel de Cervantes	86
12	Be Patient *The Odyssey* by Homer	93
13	Balance the Tactical with the Strategic *The Art of War* by Sun Tzu	105
14	Mentor Willingly *To Kill a Mockingbird* by Harper Lee	113
15	Know the Borders *Catch-22* by Joseph Heller	120
16	Deal with Loss *Beloved* by Toni Morrison	126
17	Understand the Process *The Caine Mutiny* by Herman Wouk	132
18	Never Lose Your Temper *The Quiet Warrior* by Thomas Buell	139

19	Delegate Freely *Nimitz at War* by Craig Symonds	147
20	Never Obsess *All the Pretty Horses* by Cormac McCarthy	156
21	Deal in Hope *Candide* by Voltaire	162
22	Know Your Profession *The United States Navy* by Capt. Edward L. Beach, USN (Ret.)	170
23	See the Danger *Nineteen Eighty-Four* by George Orwell	178
24	Reach for Glory Carefully *The Great Gatsby* by F. Scott Fitzgerald	187
25	Understand the History *The Guns of August* by Barbara Tuchman	196

Conclusion: What's on YOUR Bookshelf?   204

INTRODUCTION

I have always loved books. Wherever I have been in the world—on the bridge of a rolling ship during the long seagoing years of my Navy career, in the quiet dean's office of the Fletcher School of Law and Diplomacy at Tufts University in Boston, in my current office at the Carlyle Group in Washington, in the chairman's office of the Rockefeller Foundation, or at home in Florida—I always have a stack of books at hand. I can't wait to finish the one I am reading to get on to the next.

Partly this is because of how I spent my early years. My father, a career U.S. Marine Corps officer, was assigned in Athens, Greece, in the 1960s, and so it was there I lived as a young boy. There was no English-language television available in the three years we were there, so books became my escape. Both my parents, especially my mother, were inveterate readers who ensured I never developed the television habit; even today I seldom turn on anything but news programming.

I love books most because they help me learn, allow me to live a thousand different lives, and challenge me to make the best decisions. Let me explain . . .

First and most important, for me, books have always been the easiest and best way to learn. I am a deeply curious person, and long, long before the appearance of the Internet I loved to sit in a library with thousands of books surrounding me, searching for answers to questions big and small. Today, that kind of curiosity can be satisfied with a few flicks of the fingers on a smart phone; but we should remember that all the knowledge of the world has been stacked up, century by century, in book after book after book. The facts that drive the world come to us through literature. I learn best and most efficiently by reading.

Books are also for me the best means of transporting myself to an entirely different world, a different life, and a different set of challenges and rewards. A reader opening the pages of *Sharpe's Trafalgar* by Bernard Cornwall is instantly back in 1805 on the fiery deck of His Majesty's Ship *Victory* watching the Battle of Trafalgar unfold, seeing Vice Admiral Lord Nelson shot down by a French sniper, watching him carried to the cockpit to die in the moment of his greatest triumph. By opening Henry Kissinger's memoirs, another reader can stand alongside the secretary of state as he is pitching President Richard Nixon on the decision to open China. And either reader can this very afternoon go to sea in a tiny skiff with Cuban fisherman Santiago and learn that a man can be destroyed but not defeated when they pick up *The Old Man and the Sea* by Ernest Hemingway.

Finally, I believe every book I open is a simulator. By reading of the situations facing protagonists, both in fact and in fiction, I can ask myself that vital question: what would *I* do? So often, in the biggest decisions of our lives, the right answer is not crystal clear. By placing ourselves in the protagonist's mind we can effectively practice making those difficult choices. In *The Godfather* by Mario Puzo, Don Vito Corleone says to his headstrong son, Santino, that we should not make the mistake of hating our enemies, because hatred clouds our judgment. Is that always true? Can we not hold a righteous hatred for an implacable enemy—Hitler or the Islamic State, for example—without clouding our judgment?

Only by diving into literature can you put yourself in those simulated moments and mentally explore how to make the right decisions for yourself.

On and on, we can voyage on the great sea of fact and fiction, of reliable and unreliable narrators, of historical novels and voluminous biographies, afloat on the endless ocean of truly good books. And as we do, we learn about the vast and endless world; we escape and are entertained by the infinite variety of times, places, and people we encounter; and we practice and hone our own skills as strategists, decision makers, and judges of the human condition.

All this for the price of a library card—which is generally free, and these days usually has online options.

Sounds too good to be true, right? But the catch, the hard part, is deceptively simple: picking out the good books and deciding what to read. In that regard, my advice is to cast a wide net and "read fast to read slow."

As to casting a wide net, I mean learning as much about the books available to you as you can. There are thousands of volumes published each year, vastly more than any reader can conquer, and so reviews—short, readable summaries and judgments about newly published books—are the first way to narrow your list. Immensely helpful, and a primary source of recommendations, are the reviews that appear in leading newspapers and journals. If you are a specialized reader, say in maritime affairs, as I am, you will want to peruse the journals that specialize in your area of interest; for example, the U.S. Naval Institute *Proceedings* for all things dealing with the oceans. But regardless of your specialization, you should also be scanning the wider-scope journals like the *New York Times, Washington Post*, and *Wall Street Journal* for their weekly literary reviews.

Discussing books with friends who are readers can be a huge help. Local book club organizers are always diehard readers, and every good reader has a circle of friends for recommendations. One fellow four-star admiral, Harry Harris, collects signed first editions and has given me dozens of first-rate recommendations over the long years of our friendship. Similarly, good friend former Secretary of the Navy Richard Danzig, for whom I worked over the course of two eventful years in the Pentagon, is a wonderful source of book ideas. Barbara Immergut, a former editor, is a close friend and book recommender. I hear about books from neighbors, colleagues at work, and people I meet at dinner parties—and I always ask, "What are you reading?"

The proprietors of independent bookstores—which often highlight recommendations from their staff members—are a terrific source of book ideas. Some of the best recommendations I've received over the years have come from the small but mighty local indie The BookMark in Neptune Beach, Florida. When I'm in New York City, I always visit the vast Strand bookstore in Manhattan and see what their team is recommending. Ditto in south Florida at Raptis Rare Books.

Finally, the wide net you cast should include online lists of good books, and here the sources are almost infinite. You can find what celebrities and former presidents and captains of industry and entertainers are reading. Just as easily, you can look at the recommended reading lists of leaders of many huge business organizations or the military services or university leaders. Simply plugging "book recommendations" into a browser will generate literally millions of ideas and lists—I did it on Google moments ago and had 100 million hits.

The second idea worth exploring is "reading fast to read slow." What I mean by this is that to cover the most ground in reading, you need to expose yourself to lots and lots of books—skimming them, beginning them, and then being willing to discard them if they are not interesting or do not meet your needs.

There are simply too many books to do otherwise. Voltaire said the tragedy of reading was that you could begin in the first alcove of the French national library, read steadily, and die before completing even that relatively small section. So many books, so little time. Thus, I advocate picking up hundreds of books, skimming them quickly, and then identifying the handful that are meaningful, indeed crucial, to your own voyage in life.

That's when you read slow; you read carefully, taking notes to preserve what you learn. The best way to "read fast to read slow" is to use libraries (especially online) to access numerous books. Check out a big pile, work through them quickly, and pick out the few that are worth reading closely. Keeping a reader's journal is helpful—jotting down the many titles you encounter but writing seriously only about the handful of volumes that taught you something important. Your notes will help you remember what you have learned.

All of which brings us to Why *this* list? Why am I suggesting the books in *The Admiral's Bookshelf*? What I hope makes this slim offering of twenty-five books both unique and interesting is that they represent the nexus of reading and leading.

I've already done a couple of previous books along these lines (*The Leader's Bookshelf* and *The Sailor's Bookshelf*), but those were longer compilations of fifty books each, and each had a different purpose. *The Leader's Bookshelf* was compiled by synthesizing the book choices of dozens of very senior military officers. The book choices were not tied to actual principles of leadership but instead were books that inspired those leaders to be better people.

The Sailor's Bookshelf is very focused on the maritime world and was intended to help readers better understand the sea. While I stand by the value of the hundred or so books in those two volumes, neither focuses specifically on "how to lead," as this new volume does.

What I've set out to do in *The Admiral's Bookshelf* is to tie together very specific life lessons and principles of leadership that have stood me in great stead over the years with specific books that illustrate those principles for me. I've chosen twenty-five principles of life and leadership that have been fundamental for me as a military officer, a teacher and dean of a graduate school, an international business leader, and chairman of a large global philanthropic foundation. While the challenges and circumstances of each of those portions of my life and career were very different, the basic principles of life and leadership aligned quite well across the different environments. These twenty-five direct and simple ideas are almost always easy to say but hard to execute. The books I cite in this work are the keys to understanding and executing those principles.

This is not, by the way, a sappy, cheerleader-style self-help book. The books I've selected reflect both positive and negative experiences that have shaped my life. Some of them, such as *The Handmaid's Tale* and *The Old Man and the Sea*, are relatively dark. And while the list is not directly informed by my life on the oceans, my experiences at sea are part of this voyage.

As an example, a book I come back to again and again for its simple, direct, and meaningful leadership and life lessons is Colin Powell's *It Worked for Me*, essentially a collection of anecdotes and advice. In *The Admiral's Bookshelf* I've tied that book to something very specific that defined General Powell in one important way: his willingness to be his own spokesman. When the United States liberated Kuwait by attacking Iraq in the first Gulf War, General Powell, then the chairman of the Joint Chiefs, took the podium himself to brief the American public. Indeed, throughout his storied career—Army general, national security advisor, chairman of the Joint Chiefs of Staff, and ultimately secretary of state, Colin Powell personally briefed the public, the

Department of Defense and the rest of the U.S. government, and the world.

This set of connections—of life and leadership principles with selected books—creates a unique approach to reading and leading. It illustrates my own belief that the best leaders are also readers, because they have broadened their horizons through exposure to thousands of books, practiced their craft in the simulators of published volumes, and expanded their knowledge much further than simple experience alone can provide, no matter how extraordinary their life and journey.

Another way to think of this is to recognize that no *one* of us can be as smart as *all* of us thinking together. By picking the best books, by tying them consciously to the principles of life and leadership that matter the most, and by welding all of these ideas into a capable strategy for leading organizations—whether a three-person team at a small tech startup or 2 million servicemen and women in the NATO alliance—leaders can and will succeed.

Let's get under way!

CHAPTER ONE

NEVER SURRENDER

The Old Man and the Sea

by Ernest Hemingway

> But man is not made for defeat. A man can
> be destroyed but not defeated.

I cannot begin to imagine all the times I have recommended *The Old Man and the Sea* to a reader. It is a foundational book for me, going back to the first time I read it, when I was a teenager in the early 1970s. The story of Santiago, the Cuban fisherman, is a deceptively simple tale. In addition to the commonly recognized themes of resilience and character, the book is also full of lessons about mentorship, what generations owe to each other, and what we should truly value in our lives.

The arc of the story is seemingly uncomplex: an aged fisherman in Cuba, a legend in his youth, has fallen on very hard times. He lives in a one-room shack now, and when he goes out to fish in his small skiff, he is unlucky. The young boy he has mentored in the fishing profession is forced by his parents to work in another boat, although the youngster still loyally visits and brings food, beer, and newspapers—the latter so Santiago can follow his beloved American baseball.

As the story begins, Santiago goes to sea by himself as usual, but miraculously, he catches the biggest gamefish he has ever seen. After a monumental struggle that carries the skiff far out to sea, he kills the fish and secures it to the side of his boat to bring it back to port. It will be a triumphant moment of redemption after a long string of failures. But sharks, scenting blood in the water, attack the corpse of the fish where it hangs on the side of the small boat.

Over the course of the long night, they hit again and again, and slowly, surely they destroy the fish, until nothing remains but the skeleton. Santiago does all he can to fight them off, but he knows the inevitable outcome will be the destruction of the fish, and with it his dreams of fame and success. And yet he persists. As Hemingway—who clearly felt in many ways like Santiago at times during the course of his long and complicated life—said in describing the moment, "A man can be destroyed, but not defeated."

> ## "But man is not made for defeat."

I've read the novel perhaps a dozen times over the years, in good times and bad. It always provided a new thought or suggestion about how to live my life. It can be read with equal enjoyment and inspiration by a fourteen-year-old or those in their sixties, and each reading brings more of the reader's life voyage to the tale.

The moment the book literally came to life for me occurred about twenty years after I first read it. In the early 1990s I took command at sea for the first time. My warship was USS *Barry*, a brand-new guided missile destroyer. As the ship's second commanding officer, I had the enormous privilege of taking *Barry* forward for her maiden deployment overseas. With a crew of 350 and a powerful range of combat capability, *Barry* had every bit of technology available to mariners at the time.

That first deployment was extraordinary—full of remarkable experiences, including enforcing an arms blockade off the coast of the Balkans as a genocidal war raged there. We also sprinted at full speed—over thirty knots—across the eastern Mediterranean, through the Suez Canal and the Red Sea, and on to the Arabian Gulf when Saddam Hussein made yet another attempt to invade Kuwait.

There were also moments of great emotional significance for me, such as anchoring off Omaha Beach at Normandy and observing sunrise on the fiftieth anniversary of D-Day. We had spent the previous day passing in review before Her Majesty Queen Elizabeth II along with dozens of other warships, including the aircraft carrier USS *George Washington*. The poignancy of the moment when we gazed up at the legendary Pont du Hoc, where U.S. Rangers had scaled the cliffs under withering German fire, and saw to left and right of us warships of all the Allied nations anchored before the beaches, remains difficult to describe.

After more than six months forward deployed and sailing nearly forty thousand nautical miles, we returned to homeport in Norfolk, Virginia. Given the success of the deployment, *Barry* and her crew were nominated for the prestigious Battenberg Cup, awarded annually to the top ship in the Atlantic fleet. We competed against close to two hundred ships—aircraft carriers, nuclear submarines, and Aegis cruisers—and, incredibly, won the award. When the fleet commander came and presented it to my crew we were on top of the world.

But within a few weeks it all came crashing down. Like Santiago the fisherman, I felt the bitter taste of failure.

We had a long-scheduled engineering inspection, which we felt very comfortable facing. The Operational Propulsion Plant Examination (OPPE) entails an aggressive investigation into every element of a ship's engineering spaces. A team of about a dozen highly experienced naval engineers came on board on a Monday morning and dove into everything from our heat stress precautions to the level of noise in the spaces and how well we protected our Sailors.

Even more important, they began a series of material checks on the seven huge gas turbines that provided our propulsion and electricity. The inspectors looked at every inch of the piping, the insulation, cleanliness, gauges, instruments, and control systems. Everywhere they went, our Sailors accompanied them, and the inspectors quizzed them about their duties and abilities.

For the captain of the ship, the OPPE is a nerve-wracking experience. I spent the time fielding reports from my own engineers, who were constantly trying to understand how the inspectors were judging the ship. And every minute of those long days, I knew my own career and command reputation were on the line. I was confident we would succeed, as we had done for all the other operations and inspections.

> "Calm down, Jim, this is nothing compared to a combat deployment."

But failing an OPPE is almost always an immediate "relief for cause," meaning in simplest terms that the captain is summarily fired.

After a tense day in port, we got under way the next morning. As we sailed out of Norfolk harbor into the open sea, the Gulf Stream hit us hard on the starboard side and we found ourselves rolling in a difficult squall. *Not a good omen*, I thought as we began preps for the heart of the inspection: the full power trial. This is a maneuver designed to put maximum stress on the entire ship's engineering plant. We had to get to top speed essentially immediately, maintain it for a set length of time, and provide constant monitoring of the entire plant.

As we kicked the ship into high gear, I got a frantic call from my engineering officer of the watch: our lubricating oil system was failing—and failing catastrophically. The lube oil sample, which should have been clear and bright, was cloudy, almost smoky looking. We had to stop immediately and lock that shaft, change the entire batch of lube oil—hundreds of gallons—and then try again to get to full speed.

My stomach dropped, knowing we were on the edge of a bad failure. After changing the lube oil, we accelerated again, holding our collective breaths, and tested the lube oil—and it failed again.

This was mission failure. The chief inspector shook his head and told me to lock the shaft and call a tug alongside to bring *Barry* back to port. Slowly, gingerly, we limped home from sea. The rest of the fleet saw the slow speed and the tug alongside and knew we had failed the inspection. I had never felt such a moment of personal and professional failure. I called my boss—the commodore of the destroyer squadron to which I was assigned—and told him we had failed the inspection. There was a long pause on the other end of the line. Finally he said, "I'll come down at 0800 and we'll see what we need to do." His tone was ominous, and deservedly so.

I went home that night to my wife, Laura, and told her the news. I assured her I would be fired the following morning. We would figure out our future together—but it would not be in the U.S. Navy. Like Santiago the fisherman, I was destroyed. The career I'd built was ruined, and I was facing an uncertain future. Almost automatically I picked up my copy of *The Old Man and the Sea*, a battered, dog-eared, and marked-up paperback I'd kept since junior high school. And I thought to myself, *I will not be defeated—there are other worlds than the Navy.*

Of course, you will guess how the story came out for me. The next morning, my copy of *The Old Man and the Sea* in my backpack, I drove slowly to the ship, anticipating that by the end of the day I would be destroyed, my career ended, on the beach with the skeleton of my career being picked over by scavenging birds. But three things happened.

First, my commodore was surprisingly forgiving. He said, in effect, "Stavridis, bad day. Really bad day. But you've done well and we're going to give you another crack at the inspection. You'll get a down-check on your fitness report, of course, but you can overcome that. Go fix your ship, Cap'n." And he walked off.

And my crew—I thought I would spend the day pumping up a sad and depressed lot. Instead, as I walked a shell-shocked ship that day, members of the crew came up to me. Many of them patted me on the back, saying, "It's OK, Cap'n. We got this. We can do this." I was amazed and humbled by their trust and resilience.

Perhaps best of all, my peers and contemporaries on the waterfront began to call with offers of help. "Jim, bad day. Really bad day. But what can we do to help? Do you need spare parts? More lube oil? Can my master chief come over and help with training? Whatever you need, just ask." Many were Naval Academy classmates; all were helpful and kind.

As I look back on that day, I know that my commodore, my crew, and my peers all contributed to getting me through the most dangerous moment of my career, when I felt destroyed, if not defeated. But part of how I navigated those choppy seas—the worst in my career other than time in combat—was based on reading *The Old Man and the Sea*. I am literally an old man now and a long way from the sea, but still I return to that book again and again.

As a Greek American, I'm required to have a reference to Greek mythology in all my writing, so here is one for this book: Sisyphus, condemned by the gods to roll a boulder up a hill that always, just as he approaches the summit, rolls down again. I think of that myth sometimes, knowing that for every one of us, that boulder will eventually roll down.

So, the question is not whether the boulder will roll down—we know that it will. The question is, are you willing to put your shoulder to the stone, again and again and again, and begin pushing it back to the summit?

That journey, that voyage, if you'll permit me a naval metaphor, lies ahead for us all. I recommend *The Old Man and the Sea* as a companion for anyone sailing a hard sea.

CHAPTER TWO

PICK THE RIGHT PEOPLE

The Godfather

by Mario Puzo

> I respect those who tell me the truth
> no matter how hard it is.

I believe that *The Godfather* is one of the great American novels, of a piece with *Moby-Dick* by Herman Melville and *Blood Meridian* by Cormac McCarthy. *Moby-Dick* is about personal ambition and obsession, as well as humans' long relationship with the sea. *Blood Meridian* is about the lawless and violent American West. In *The Godfather*, Mario Puzo gives us a novel of the American immigrant experience—and so much more. It is a master work on leadership, full of powerful and accurate lessons about how to run an effective and efficient enterprise, albeit in this case a criminal one. In many ways it is a modern version of Machiavelli's Renaissance masterpiece, *The Prince*. It is no coincidence, by the way, that Puzo also wrote powerfully about the Borgia family of Machiavelli's time.

Many Americans, of course, have seen the masterful film trilogy directed by Francis Ford Coppola, starring Al Pacino as Michael, the rising star of the Corleone family, Marlon Brando as the wise and wily Godfather Don Vito, James Caan as the hotheaded oldest son, Santino ("Sonny"), and Robert De Niro as the young Don Vito. A superb performance by Robert Duvall as the family's unconventional Irish consigliere rounds out one of the most talented film casts ever assembled. The quality of the three films varies, with the second widely regarded as the best and the third and final segment as of distinctly lesser quality—but in all three films, and certainly in the novel itself, leadership lessons abound.

The story of the Corleone family begins with the arrival of young Vito to a bustling New York City in the early part of the twentieth century. Through will and ruthless determination, the impoverished orphan builds an enterprise on the streets, gathering a group of fellow Sicilians and establishing both a legitimate olive oil business and a powerful crime family. At the time the original novel, *The Godfather*, opens, just after World War II, the crime family is wildly successful. The Godfather controls many politicians and law enforcement officials and owns a sprawling estate.

Vito Corleone falls from power and is almost assassinated by a rival family when he rejects a business proposal that would have required him to go against his personal code of honor. Santino recruits Michael, the Don's youngest son, to carry out a revenge killing of the gangster who attacked the Don. Michael accomplishes the deed and immediately flees to Sicily. A subsequent gang war led by Santino wreaks havoc on the family business, results in Santino's death, and most of the other characters suffer painful losses.

Throughout it all, the Don maintains his fundamental principles of leadership. He keeps a calm head despite all the turmoil around him; displays plenty of physical courage and a strategic sense of how to, in time, conquer his enemies; and takes a philosophical approach that ultimately allows him to turn the family over to Michael. We see him call on the many people for whom he has done favors over the years ("Someday, and that day may never come, I will call upon you to do a service for me."). The Don is patient and philosophical ("Forgive. Forget. Life is full of misfortunes.") and waits to have his way.

> **"Revenge is a dish best served cold."**

He knows that one must think with one's head, not one's heart ("Never hate your enemies. It affects your judgment."). Many of these pearls of wisdom, by the way, echo sentiments that appeared in *The Prince* nearly four centuries earlier.

But above all else, Don Corleone is a master at judging the people he wants on his team. Again and again he speaks of competence and having the highest-quality and most trustworthy people around him.

> **"I want reliable people, people who aren't going to be carried away."**

Throughout the novel, which is ultimately a meditation on power and leadership, Don Corleone shows us—perhaps ironically, given the business he is in—that the best leaders are those who consistently invest in their people, and do so honestly and with their eyes wide open. ("You have to take time and trouble [with subordinates]").

That leadership lesson truly became clear for me when I worked for one of the most demanding American leaders of the early twenty-first century, Secretary of Defense Donald Rumsfeld. I was selected to be his senior military assistant in 2004, as I was completing several years at sea in command of a carrier strike group based on the nuclear aircraft carrier USS *Enterprise*—a big command with thousands of Sailors and a dozen ships. We had just returned from a long forward deployment into combat in Iraq and Afghanistan in the early days of what has come to be called the "forever wars."

I got a call from the Chief of Naval Operations, Adm. Vern Clark, who told me I would be the Navy's nominee for the three-star vice admiral job. When I pointed out that I was only a one-star rear admiral, the CNO said, "Believe me, if you convince Don Rumsfeld you're the right person for the job, he will promote you directly to three stars." I wasn't aware that was even possible, but I didn't think I had much of a chance at the job anyway when I went into his office to interview. We hit it off surprisingly well, and over the next couple of years I learned an enormous amount from the famously demanding and difficult secretary.

It was a high-tempo assignment, and despite wearing three stars, I was in the Pentagon before 5 a.m. each morning and often still there well into the evening hours. I joked with my wife that at least I didn't need sunglasses to work for Secretary Rumsfeld. From him I learned about the challenges of working with the staffers and politicians on Capitol Hill (he had a particular animosity for Navy hero Senator John McCain, which made my life difficult), how to drive the interagency process (where we competed with Secretary Colin Powell at the State Department and National Security Advisor Condoleezza Rice, among others), and the intricacies of running a huge bureaucracy with a budget in excess of $600 billion and 3 million personnel.

I failed early and often to meet Secretary Rumsfeld's expectations. He was simply impossible to fully please on just about any project. One of his favorite aphorisms about himself was "I've been blessed with an eye for a flaw," and again and again he exercised that skill. He was also preternaturally energetic, often going home from work with two briefcases stuffed with documents that would be returned to us the next day full of corrections, rewrites, and big scrawled notices of his dissatisfaction. I thought I'd get fired in a few months and started to daydream about life after the Navy.

Gradually, however, I got a better sense of Rumsfeld, and my performance improved. I certainly used the lessons of *The Old Man and the Sea* in terms of steeling myself day after day to be resilient and to try my best—even as I met with defeat in many aspects of my job. But all along I was learning from Rumsfeld, who had led an exceptional life—Navy pilot, member of Congress, White House chief of staff, previous term as secretary of defense, CEO of Fortune 500 companies, and ambassador. You can learn a lot from someone like that.

The biggest lesson I learned from Rumsfeld came right out of *The Godfather*. It had to do with picking the right people. Rumsfeld had a theory, and I think he was largely right, that a leader who was somewhat insecure would hire people he or she could dominate. A weak leader didn't want someone who would tell them unpleasant truths. Such people tend to be afraid of bad news, and their insecurity makes them surround themselves with fawning, subservient subordinates.

On the other hand, confident, bold leaders surround themselves with people who can truly challenge them. I often saw the secretary reject a candidate for an important position because the person agreed with him a bit too easily and instead pick someone who challenged one of his assumptions. He applied that filter invariably, and as a result the inner team around him tended to be a bit quirky, certainly self-confident, and perhaps not always the "push" candidate submitted by each of the services.

Secretary Rumsfeld would say that "As hire As and Bs hire Cs," meaning that the best leaders go for the truth-telling, creative-thinking, risk-taking A players around them rather than looking for yes-men and -women. The people surrounding Vladimir Putin are a good case in point—as weak a collection of C and D players as I've ever met, and I've met many of them. Putin keeps them around because he knows that neither collectively nor individually do they have the skills or the courage to challenge him and his (obviously flawed) assumptions. That philosophy, by the way, is central to his massive strategic miscalculation in invading Ukraine in February 2022.

Whenever I heard Don Rumsfeld opine on his hiring philosophy (which he did frequently), I would smile and think of *The Godfather*. Both Rumsfeld and Don Vito not only hired the best and were unafraid to be challenged by their subordinates, but they also spent an inordinate amount of time on personnel matters. Rumsfeld, for example, devoted dozens of hours monthly—a huge investment of his time while he was dealing with enormous wars in Iraq and Afghanistan—in making personnel choices. He hired a retired three-star vice admiral, Staser Holcomb, to act as his personal in-house personnel consultant and advisor. He personally interviewed every single officer nominated for a three- or four-star assignment, again a huge time commitment.

Similarly, the fictional Don Vito, from the time he began assembling his "family" in New York City, surrounded himself with the very best subordinates, including the young Irishman

Tom Hagen who became his consigliere, an unheard-of choice for a role a fellow Sicilian should have filled. And he invested constantly in the lives and careers of his three completely different sons: hotheaded Sonny, hapless Fredo, and cold, calculating Michael. He understood how important that kind of investment in personnel was for any organization: "The strength of a family, like the strength of an army, lies in its loyalty to each other."

> "Great men are not born great, they grow great."

Those are smart precepts, and in my time as a commander I tried hard to follow them. In every one of my flag assignments, I insisted to my staff that I wanted to spend at least a quarter of my time on personnel matters. That was hard, because the competing demands—operational matters, innovation and new ideas, and strategic communications—were vitally important as well. But the time you take as a leader to pick the right people will not only serve you in the immediate moment but will benefit your organization over the long term. Don Vito's choice to elevate Michael to be his successor, for example, something neither of them wanted initially, echoed on in the family well beyond the next generation. The choices Don Rumsfeld made in selecting a generation of three- and four-stars benefited the Department of Defense for a decade and more.

I've read *The Godfather* several times over the years as I've matured in my own leadership skills, and each time I read it the book speaks some new truth to me. I often quote it, prefacing it by saying, only slightly tongue-in-cheek, "I'm about to tell you something from the greatest book of leadership ever written." When I mention *The Godfather*, people are almost always surprised and skeptical. Partly that is because the novel is also a gripping narrative full of drama, surprise twists, and a fair amount of sex and violence. I never asked Don Rumsfeld what he thought of it, or even if he'd read it, but in many of the decisions he made, the secretary did indeed choose the best people. And while Don Rumsfeld's tenure, like Don Vito's, was quite controversial, I am confident that his successes—and there were many—were largely a result of his laser focus on picking good subordinates. That is a powerful leadership lesson, and one that echoes from the Italian Renaissance of Machiavelli and Cesare Borgia in *The Prince* to the tales of a fictional twentieth-century Mafia family to the halls of the Kremlin and the White House today.

CHAPTER THREE

BE YOUR OWN SPOKESMAN
It Worked for Me
by Colin Powell

For my press appearances, I identified five prominent audiences: reporters, the American people, political and military leaders in other countries, the enemy (who is watching), and the troops.

I met Colin Powell in Washington in the fall of 1991 when I was a very young Navy commander, fresh out of combat in the Arabian Gulf during Operation Desert Shield/Desert Storm, and he was the chairman of the Joint Chiefs of Staff. General Powell came to the National War College—of which he was a proud alumnus—to give a talk to my class of around a hundred students.

His remarks were memorable for several reasons, most notably because he took off his tie to "get comfortable" before he started. I'd seen more than my share of senior officers over the course of my various Pentagon and Washington tours, and not one of them had ever taken off their tie, at least not when speaking in front of a big group of officers. He was utterly relaxed, very confident without being the least bit arrogant, and quite funny. At one point he said, "People accuse me of being a 'political general.' Guilty." He pointed at his chest. "I've had multiple tours in the building [the Pentagon], worked in the White House, and been a White House Fellow. I'm proud of it."

At this point in his career—as the apex officer in the armed forces—he was certainly entitled to feel confident. And what is more important, he was coming off the most successful U.S. military operation since the end of World War II, the first Gulf War. The U.S. armed forces destroyed Saddam Hussein's armies in the deserts of Iraq in a matter of days. That campaign remains in my view the most perfect large-scale military operation in American history—short, sharp, decisive, and brilliantly executed. It exorcised the ghosts of Vietnam (which, sadly, have reemerged post-Afghanistan) and firmly validated the concept of joint operations.

After the talk, a very small group of about a dozen of us who were National Defense University Fellows (designated to work on special research projects during our year at NDU) had almost an hour with the chairman in what turned out to be a seminar on leadership. He started by asking each of us to say something about ourselves. As the only Navy officer in the group, I got special attention from General Powell, including the comment, "Stavridis, I know you're the smartest guy in the room because you didn't go to West Point." (He was a proud graduate of the City College of New York, having grown up in the Bronx, the son of Jamaican immigrants.) As he left after the talk, he asked us to keep in touch, and I did.

Over the next several decades, I would try to drop by his office, wherever it was, for a brief courtesy call. Sometimes he was too busy to accommodate me, but most times he was willing. I would sit with him for half an hour, or even an hour, and tell him what was happening in my career, about my small victories and defeats, happy to gain his advice. As I ascended through the ranks of the Navy, he continued to mentor me. I treasure a signed, limited edition of his extraordinary memoir, *An American Life*, which I've read twice.

Before I departed for my final tour in uniform to be the sixteenth Supreme Allied Commander of NATO, we spent a full hour together in his house. He had left government service at that point after serving as secretary of state. Colin Powell knew world affairs intimately, of course, but that afternoon he talked about the Balkan Wars and explained how military force had been intertwined with diplomacy to create the settlements that ended that long and vicious conflict. He spoke very bluntly about the challenges of dealing with the NATO bureaucracy in general and the Supreme Allied Commander in particular. Fortunately, I took detailed notes, because I referred to them many times during my tenure in command of NATO. I remember looking down through the glass top of the coffee table between us and seeing his Presidential Medal of Freedom, and realizing, not for the first time, that I was in the presence of a truly exceptional American.

At the end of the conversation, he sat back in his chair, took a final sip of coffee, and said, "Jim, you are going to do fine over there. Just remember, we aren't sending you to Europe to be Charlemagne." Meaning, keep your ego in check, Stavridis. I suspect he had seen too many Supreme Allied Commanders overfocus on the first word of their title—which is, in fact, a damn good title. "Sir, I'm not tall enough to be Charlemagne,"

I replied, and he laughed and stood to shake my hand. He was a leader's leader, and I often think of him and remember his advice on so many different things.

Here's the good news: even now that General Powell (and he'll always be a general, not a cabinet secretary, in the eyes of the military) is deployed to heaven, everyone can get a healthy dose of his advice in the unique and lovely small book of leadership he wrote with the deceptively simple title, *It Worked for Me*. The only books I can compare it to are the classic volume of intrigue and power, *The Prince* by Machiavelli, and *Rumsfeld's Rules* (quite an irony considering that Powell and Rumsfeld were often bitter policy opponents).

General Powell's book works on many levels. It captures, in a series of vignettes and aphorisms, a philosophy of life, a rich bouquet of leadership lessons, and some very funny anecdotes, and functions also as a poignant reminiscence of his times. Slender as it is, the book manages to distill the essence of his journey: he was born to Jamaican immigrants in New York in the mid-1930s, educated in the public City College of New York funded by an ROTC scholarship, and spent thirty-five eventful years as a soldier. Along the way he had many unusual jobs and experiences—the "political general"—including senior military assistant to the secretary of defense (a job I later held for Don Rumsfeld), national security advisor, and of course chairman of the Joint Chiefs of Staff. Perhaps most famously to the public, he served several difficult years as the secretary of state in the turbulent George W. Bush administration.

He was instrumental in what is perhaps America's most important victory: the Cold War. And in addition to the success of the Gulf War, he oversaw another brilliant military success in the invasion of Panama, which brought to justice the dictator Manual Noriega. He managed a couple dozen different military crises and interventions and created what we still call the Powell Doctrine, which in essence limits military response unless such action would enjoy the sincere support of the American public, has overwhelming force at hand, and satisfies a core U.S. security interest. A career soldier, he was passionate about the need for diplomacy to solve crises and to resolve the long-term challenges we face in international politics.

One of the core pieces of advice he gave me along the way, which echoes through *It Worked for Me*, is something many leaders find difficult to do: be your own spokesman.

> "Be your own spokesman."

In a moment I will always remember, during the first Gulf War, as chairman of the Joint Chiefs, he stood at the lectern and briefed the operation personally. He knew that a crucial moment in the history of the U.S. military was unfolding, and no one was more aware of the ghosts still in the room from the war in Vietnam, where he fought and was wounded.

Colin Powell understood instinctively that the leader must fully own moments like that. And he was able to use all that he had learned in his long voyage to the very top of the U.S. military to good effect. He stood in front of the maps and charts and said simply, "Our strategy to go after this army is very, very simple. First, we're going to cut it off, and then we're going to kill it." He was talking about an army of about half a million soldiers. And that was exactly what the U.S. military did.

Leaders must be unafraid to stand and deliver under pressure, knowing that if things go south, they will be the ones who carry the responsibility. That was one of the most important lessons I learned from General Powell.

It Worked for Me is more generally a primer on the broad principles of leadership that the general stood for. I would note that of his powerful thirteen pieces of advice cited below, four are about optimism. Wherever I have been in the world, whatever my responsibilities, great or small, I've tried to follow these ideals. And I've tried to follow Powell's example by explaining the plan to my team and talking about it publicly—and then be ready to take the consequences, both good and bad.

- It ain't as bad as you think! It will look better in the morning.
- Get mad, then get over it.
- Avoid having your ego so close to your position that when your position falls, your ego goes with it.
- It can be done.
- Be careful what you choose. You may get it.
- Don't let adverse facts stand in the way of a good decision.
- You can't make someone else's choices. You shouldn't let someone else make yours.
- Check small things.
- Share credit.
- Remain calm. Be kind.
- Have a vision. Be demanding.
- Don't take counsel of your fears or naysayers.
- Perpetual optimism is a force multiplier.

I wish I could say I was as good on a podium as Colin Powell, but I wasn't. As a briefer, for years I used densely packed PowerPoint slides, in the classic Pentagon style. I was nervous and tended to compensate by pouring on too much depth, as if trying to show the audience how smart I was. I gradually got better, but I never mastered the skill to the degree that General Powell did, although I can't think of a higher bar to get over.

We lost General Powell a couple of years ago, but he lives on for me in his spirit and wisdom in ways that few others do. The last time I saw him was just before the pandemic at an Alfalfa Club dinner, one of Washington's sillier traditions. He was standing on the other side of the room surrounded by a half-dozen people listening to him with smiles on their faces. Laughter broke out frequently as I walked toward him. The leadership seminar continued. I miss him still.

Read *It Worked for Me* to be a part of that leadership seminar. You won't regret it.

CHAPTER FOUR

WRITE WITH SIMPLICITY AND PRECISION

The Elements of Style
by William Strunk Jr. and E. B. White

> I treasure *The Elements of Style* for its sharp advice, but I treasure it even more for its audacity and self-confidence.
>
> —E. B. White, 1979

I first encountered this tiny volume when I was a midshipman entering the U.S. Naval Academy in 1972, more than half a century ago. It was inside the seabag of uniforms, instruments (from a slide rule to a sextant), and books each midshipman fourth class received on induction day. The cover of the paperback copy I was given was light blue, like the ocean's surface on a sunny day. Visually, this was a small relief given that the school's colors were vivid gold and dark navy blue. It was almost soothing to look at that book's cover.

After we staggered back to our un-air-conditioned rooms in massive Bancroft Hall, our dormitory, home to the four thousand midshipmen of the brigade, we had a couple of hours to stow everything away. This included folding our socks in a highly prescribed manner and making sure our uniforms were hung in the closets in the correct order by season. It was mind-numbing work, but I managed to finish early and then sat on my bunk and flipped through *The Elements of Style*. For a few moments I was able to forget the rigors of plebe summer and absorb some of the sharp rhetorical commands of the book.

I will admit, the process of writing has always been fundamental to me, as important in many ways as reading. In high school, I was the editor of the McClintock *Guidon*, the school's newspaper, and I also wrote a weekly column for the local *Tempe Daily News* in central Arizona. At Annapolis, I went on to become the editor of *The Log*, the school's monthly magazine, and have since written thousands of articles and fifteen books, including this one. I've been a contributing editor of *Time* magazine and a weekly columnist for *Bloomberg Opinion*. I like to think of myself as a successful author.

But I was not self-taught. Through it all, going back to that humid midsummer day at Annapolis, *The Elements of Style* has been a go-to resource on everything from the specific commands of tricky grammar to the process of composition, to commonly misspelled words.

I still have that now very battered volume, which has accompanied me on land and sea for thousands of miles. It has had a place in the drawer of every desk I've owned, including the one in northeast Florida where I write today. Over the years, I have acquired copies of each of the now four editions. My favorite of the quartet is the 2007 fourth edition, gorgeously illustrated by the contemporary artist Maira Kalman and featuring a cover illustration of the basset hound owned by the original author, William Strunk.

When I saw the announcement that an illustrated edition would be coming out, I was skeptical. But the linking of the dozens of illustrations to the sharply ordered commands in the book is done with wit and style. For example, Strunk and White describe how to construct sentences in ways that make the most sense for readers. An example of a bad sentence provided is "He noticed a large stain in the rug that was right in the center." Next to that is an improved version: "He noticed a large stain right in the center of the rug."

The Maira Kalman illustration, which takes up the entire facing page, shows an obviously wealthy family, cocktails in hand, seated in a well-appointed family room with—in the center of the rug—a dead body in a pool of blood. The illustration solidifies the importance of word order in sentence structure; Rule 20: Keep related words together.

The book is structured in six sections, each with a handful of examples of both good and bad grammar, spelling, and composition.

Section I, "Elementary Rules of Usage," is a series of eleven very direct rules issued in clean, direct prose. As E. B. White says in his foreword to the original edition, "The reader will soon discover that these rules and principles are in the form of sharp commands, Sergeant Strunk snapping orders to his platoon." Most of them are things we learned along the voyage of education but might have forgotten or ignored.

Occasionally the commands take a bit of thought, even for word mavens like me. Take Rule 11: A participial phrase at the beginning of a sentence must refer to the grammatical subject.

But the authors provide crystal clear examples of how people can get this wrong, which can lead to ridiculous sounding sentences such as:

Incorrect: "Young and inexperienced, the task seemed easy to me."
Correct: "Young and inexperienced, I thought the task easy."

Another bad example raises the form to the near comical:

"Wondering irresolutely what to do next, the clock struck twelve."

After marching through the opening directives, Strunk and White move on to Section II, "Elementary Rules of Composition." Here we find another ten sharp commands.

I love this section and often give it a quick skim before sitting down to compose. As Roger Angell says in his foreword to the fourth edition, "Writing is hard, even for authors who do it all the time."

> **"Writing is hard, even for authors who do it all the time."**

These ten commandments, at least for composition, are as fundamental and important as those on the tablets God gave to Moses. When you pick up and read truly clean prose—say, the King James Bible or the works of Winston Churchill—you find deep adherence to the ten rules of composition. Here they are:

- Choose a suitable design and hold to it.
- Make the paragraph the unit of composition.
- Use the active voice.
- Put statements in positive form.
- Use definite, specific, and concrete language.
- Omit needless words.
- Avoid a succession of loose sentences.
- Express coordinate ideas in similar form.
- Keep related words together.
- In summaries, keep to one tense.
- Place the emphatic words of a sentence at the end.

Each of these commandments is accompanied by a simple explanation, and the entire section can be read in a few minutes. Believe me, reading them is the best way to begin any composition.

Section III is the shortest in the volume, just a couple of pages long. It lays out a "Few Matters of Form" ranging from how to use an exclamation point correctly (only after a command, like Halt!) to using hyphens properly (waterfowl, not water-fowl). A few comments on manuscripts (leave plenty of room at the top of a submission and maintain margins of a certain size) conclude this brief set of commands.

In Section IV, "Words and Expressions Commonly Misused," we find Strunk and White really cracking our collective knuckles. Some of my favorites are:

Meaningful:	A bankrupt adjective. Chose another or rephrase.
Nice:	A shaggy, all-purpose word to be used sparingly in formal composition.
In the last analysis:	A bankrupt expression.

Personalize: A pretentious word, often carrying bad advice.

This alphabetized list includes many imprecise expressions and formulations that writers should avoid.

As I've mentioned previously, one of the most demanding bosses I've ever had was two-time Secretary of Defense Donald Rumsfeld. Don was a walking edition of Strunk and White, ready to pounce at any transgression. One of his favorite corrections was to the word "unique." I learned this on my first month on the job when I tried to curry favor by handing him what I thought was a well-written paper from the staff on the necessity of a new design for our armored personnel carriers in the bloody fight in Iraq, saying, "Here you go, Mr. Secretary. This is an extremely unique set of recommendations."

He squinted over his glasses and said, "Stavridis, listen to yourself. First of all, you just got here five minutes ago, and you can't possibly have any idea about whether this is a good, bad, or indifferent set of recommendations. But more importantly, there is no such thing as 'extremely unique.' Something is either unique or it isn't. There are no gradations in the word unique." He abruptly took the paper, and I turned and walked out of his office, dismissed to grammar hell.

This sent me back to *The Elements of Style*, and sure enough, there it was, in Section IV: Unique: Means without like or equal. Hence there can be no degrees of uniqueness.

The penultimate Section V, titled "An Approach to Style (with a List of Reminders)," is to me the most useful part of the book because it encapsulates the rules for writing clean, linear prose. The first four sections of *The Elements of Style* are about what is right and what is wrong—they are black-and-white rules. But Section V is about finding a sense of style as a writer, or as the authors put it, creating prose that is "distinguished and distinguishing."

The authors freely admit that "here we leave solid ground." As a writer you may or may not agree entirely with the approach they take, but I do. I often say that the most important class I took in high school was journalism. There I learned to write simple, direct, active prose; put it in a coherent structure from the most important things to the least; construct an eye-catching first paragraph; and write under the pressure of time. Many of those ideas are folded into Section V.

It is impossible to do justice to the book in this brief chapter, but it is worth simply listing the commands. In the book, each of these suggestions is followed by a paragraph or two of explanation. Here I add in parentheses my own editorial comment to give a sense of the explanation you will find in *The Elements of Style*.

> Place yourself in the background. (Get out of your own way.)
>
> Write in a way that comes naturally. (Find and maintain your own voice.)
>
> Work from a suitable design. (Get the important points up front.)
>
> Write with nouns and verbs. (Adjectives and adverbs are spice, not bread and butter.)
>
> Revise and rewrite. (Again and again; and show your work to others frequently.)
>
> Do not overwrite. (Readers gag on ornate prose.)
>
> Do not overstate. (Audiences grow suspicious quickly.)
>
> Avoid the use of qualifiers. (So often the verb or noun is all you need.)
>
> Do not affect a breezy manner. (Write with dignity.)

Use orthodox spelling. (Amen.)

Do not explain too much. (Let conversation and examples reveal your key points.)

Do not construct awkward adverbs. (No one climbs "tiredly" up to bed.)

Make sure the reader knows who is speaking. (It's easy to lose the reader without taking constant care on this point.)

Avoid fancy words (e.g., beauteous, curvaceous, discombobulate).

Do not use dialect unless your ear is good. (Almost no one's ear is good enough.)

Be clear. (Show your writing to someone you trust but who doesn't know your subject well.)

Do not inject opinion. (Unless you are writing what is clearly an opinion piece, such as an OPED.)

Use figures of speech sparingly. (Never is a good rule.)

Do not take shortcuts at the cost of clarity. (Avoid abbreviations.)

Avoid foreign languages. (Injecting foreign phrases is often annoying and almost always unnecessary.)

Prefer the standard to the offbeat. (Don't get carried away by cool new words invented on the Internet for texting.)

Finally, Section VI provides a simple list of frequently misspelled words. In the age of automatic spellcheck and the occasionally annoying autocorrect, the list is probably less necessary than when the book appeared, but it seems a comfortable and grounded way to end this small and useful book.

I have found a dearth of good writing in each of my careers—military, education, and finance. Part of that is our failing elementary, secondary, and even undergraduate educational systems. Also responsible for that lack is writers' failure to read good writing by others, which is one of the best ways to improve. A third problem is that many bosses simply don't demand good prose (and in many cases cannot produce it themselves).

Sloppy, imprecise, and verbose writing can create real risk in every profession. Certainly in the military, precision in the way we communicate in formal message traffic, generate commands in combat, create written briefings, submit written budgets, and issue directives to the forces in the field is vital. Failure here can cause loss of life and even disaster.

In the academic world encompassing the study of international relations, and as the dean of a top graduate school, I often saw articles and papers generated by our faculty that failed to meet basic standards of accuracy and organization on topics of immense importance to the world. Bad writing can doom treaties, agreements on environmental issues, and efforts to solve diplomatic crises. And most recently in my own life in international business and finance, I see the failure of many organizations to use writing to intelligently describe their basic missions, construct sensible and convincing transaction explanations, build the case to secure funding, or conclude high-level agreements with billions of dollars at risk.

I don't want to suggest that writing is easy for me: it is not. Like most people, I struggle with putting words together in a coherent way that brings a reader along smoothly and seamlessly. There are multiple mistakes in my own published work, often things I should have corrected in earlier drafts. When I go back and read some of my early articles in professional journals, I'm embarrassed by the pompous tone of many of them. Clearly, I hadn't fully inculcated *The Elements of Style*.

Approaching writing as a critical and meaningful craft can help to solve these challenges. And that means maximizing the educational opportunities that exist; reading good, clean prose and consciously trying to emulate it; and demanding precision in writing from our shipmates in the workplace.

The Elements of Style is not a panacea for the obstacles we all face in fashioning the most effective writing, but it can help any of us immensely, both personally and within our organizations. I freely admit to occasionally violating its principles and rules, both intentionally and simply in error. But the short, tight, clear advice distilled and available here is pure gold for writers at any level. And it is a book that has deeply influenced my own life as a writer in many ways on many occasions. As Don Rumsfeld might say, it is not a unique book. We know there is no such thing. But this slim volume has helped me again and again.

CHAPTER FIVE

USE HUMOR OFTEN
A Confederacy of Dunces
by *John Kennedy Toole*

> Apparently I lack some particular perversion which today's employer is seeking.
>
> —Ignatius J. Reilly

Although born of a deep and real tragedy, this is one of the most humorous novels ever written. Hemingway said once that a man has to take a lot of punishment to write a really funny book; such is the story of *A Confederacy of Dunces*. Against the seedy southern gothic backdrop of New Orleans in the 1960s, John Kennedy Toole sets one of the most memorable characters in twentieth-century American literature. Ignatius J. Reilly is chronically unemployed, intellectually pompous, utterly misanthropic, and lives in a dysfunctional relationship with his mother. Scornful of the world around him, he is the ultimate unreliable narrator, wildly humorous without ever intending to be.

The book's title comes from a Jonathan Swift quote: "When a true genius appears in the world, you may know him by this sign, that the dunces are all in confederacy against him." Ignatius Reilly believes himself to be that genius, a man literally surrounded by a world full of dunces placed on this earth to annoy him. In that regard, it seems clear that Toole identified with his principal character and, like Ignatius, found the world a frustrating place. The ultimate tragedy in Toole's life was simple and devastating: his writing—which meant everything to him—was never appreciated in his lifetime. Publishers rejected his manuscript again and again. *A Confederacy of Dunces* ultimately achieved everything Toole wanted, even to winning the Pulitzer Prize in 1981, but it came far too late: frustrated by his lack of success, Toole had committed suicide in 1969.

I came across the novel in the early 1980s, after it won the Pulitzer Prize, while I was serving on an aircraft carrier in the Mediterranean Sea. One of the models Toole had in mind as he wrote was Joseph Heller's brilliant and tragicomic novel of World War II, *Catch 22*. Like Heller, Toole created a protagonist who uses satire, dark humor, cynicism, and comedy to confront the dunces that he believes surround him. On that battered and aging carrier, USS *Forrestal,* I found the dark humor of the book compelling. I read it on the ship's hangar deck, a huge open set of bays just below the flight deck, surrounded by the airwing's seventy planes there for maintenance and relief from the salt spray up on the flight deck.

Sitting on a bollard overlooking the placid Mediterranean, I would read a couple of chapters each day on breaks between my long watches down in the engineering spaces of the carrier, where

I served as the boilers officer. I often laughed out loud at what I read. The book provided a few weeks of both escape and comic relief from the deadly serious work of forward-deployed naval operations. Only after I finished it did I learn that the author had committed suicide before it was published. It made me sad to know that Toole would never write a sequel; but it also made me appreciate even more the genius of the writing.

I took heart from the story of how the book finally made it to print after Toole's mother, Thelma, managed to convince another superb southern writer, Walker Percy, to take up the cause. This endlessly amusing and deeply satisfying book was finally published by Louisiana State University Press in 1980. It has sold millions of copies since and has been translated into more than twenty languages. In the tragedy of Toole's suicide, the ultimate redemption of his vision for the book was realized, demonstrating the appeal of humor even when painted on a dark canvas.

The novel takes us into the mind of Ignatius Reilly, an overweight intellectual snob with an advanced degree in the history of the Middle Ages who lives with his mother, Irene. Reilly hates the dunces who populate the world around him and ends up in altercations with almost everyone he encounters. A chance confrontation with an officious police officer, told with comic overtones, ends with mother and son headed—where else—to a bar in the French Quarter. Irene overindulges and then crashes their car.

The immense repair bill forces Ignatius to return to the workforce for the first time in years. Among the jobs he takes is running a hotdog stand, where he eats more hotdogs than he sells. The running dialogue of his misanthropic interactions with the public when he is forced out into the world is uproarious. He encounters a robust cast of characters ranging from New Orleans police officers to strippers and pornographic models, to professors at nearby Tulane University. Through it all runs his fascination with Myrna Minkoff, a New Yorker of very different political inclinations.

There are profound lessons of life and leadership in *A Confederacy of Dunces*. The novel shows us that even in the darkest times, humor can be a shield and a refuge for the human spirit. Military people know this well. The history of warfare is replete with the kind of gallows humor that would have appealed to Ignatius Reilly. Humor can also be a useful tool in the worlds of business, education, medicine, the law, and many other walks of life. Again and again, I have seen the tensest situations defused by a well-timed line.

One of my favorite stories in this regard comes from the Greco-Persian wars fought more than 2,500 years ago. The Persians, under the self-anointed god-king Xerxes, sent a massive army to attack the city-states of Greece. The warlike Spartans sent a contingent of three hundred elite warriors to stop them at the narrow mountain pass at Thermopylae. The Spartan king, Leonidas, was told that the Persians had so many archers in their vast army that their arrows would blot out the rays of the sun. "So much the better," Leonidas said, "for then we will fight in the shade."

Gen. Douglas MacArthur, who commanded the Allied forces in the Pacific theater in World War II, was the source of another famous one-liner. He had become the chief of staff of the U.S. Army in 1930 and had seen significant combat earlier in his career as well. Chosen as military advisor to the Philippines by President Franklin D. Roosevelt before the war, MacArthur barely escaped from the island of Corregidor under desperate circumstances as the Japanese closed in. He received the Medal of Honor following the Philippines campaign and went on to lead U.S. forces in the Korean War. A master of the well-timed phrase, he is supposed to have commented, "Whoever said the pen is mightier than the sword obviously never encountered automatic weapons."

I'm not a combat pilot, but while commanding USS *Enterprise* and her airwing in Operation Iraqi Freedom I often dropped in to the ready rooms of the various attack squadrons to see their pre-mission briefs. These meetings are deadly serious affairs, but one of the F-18 squadrons traditionally started the mission brief with a photo of a pilot floating in a parachute toward land with a quote, supposedly from the *U.S. Air Force Operations Manual*, beneath it cautioning pilots who were forced to eject.

> **"It is generally inadvisable to eject directly over the area you just bombed."**

Colin Powell was a master of the use of humor in every situation. That is not to say he didn't take his jobs—senior military assistant to the Secretary of Defense, national security advisor, chairman of the Joint Chiefs, and secretary of state—very, very seriously; he did. But he knew that humor was essential. The quotation hanging behind his desk when I visited him as a junior officer epitomized that idea.

During the Civil War, President Lincoln received a telegram from the Union Army notifying him that the Confederate cavalry had surrounded and subdued a Union camp and captured a brigadier general and a hundred horses. "Sure hate to lose those one hundred horses," Lincoln said sadly. The telegraph operator overheard him and said, "But Mr. President, what about the brigadier general?" And Lincoln said, "I can make a brigadier general in five minutes, but it is not easy to replace one hundred horses." General Powell kept that quotation on a sign right behind his desk as a reminder to visitors.

One of my closest friends over my long years in the Navy was Doug Crowder, who retired as a vice admiral. While many senior officers decide to write a book on their leadership philosophy after retiring, Doug instead produced *Sea Stories: Humor & Life Lessons from a 40-Year Navy Journey*. This very funny volume epitomizes the need to find the humor in even the most demanding and serious moments.

One story from this fine book recounts an event that occurred when Doug was a young ensign in USS *Ramsey*. After months of hard work, he had achieved the important ship-handling and watch-standing designation as officer of the deck. His initial assignment was the morning watch from 8 a.m. to noon. He was excited and a bit scared at having the huge responsibility for the safety and navigation of a frontline Navy warship for the first time. A couple of the more senior officers on the ship "dropped by" to make sure everything was going well.

Then Doug heard the boatswain's mate of the watch call out, "Executive Officer [second in command of the ship] is on the bridge." Doug decided to ignore the exec's presence and continued simply facing forward, looking at the bow, as the officer of the deck is required to do. After a few minutes, Doug heard the exec say loudly, "Hey, Doug, is it safe to take this thing off?"

Doug turned and saw the exec, Cdr. Fritz Gaylord, sitting in the exec's chair and wearing a big, brightly colored regulation issue life jacket as though preparing to abandon ship. Everyone on the bridge burst out laughing, including the future three-star admiral. Gaylord got out of his chair, came over to Doug, and leaned in and softly said, "I'm proud of you Doug. I know you don't need any help up here." Doug would tell you he remembers that comment fifty years ago like it happened today.

It was a beautiful example of using humor to tease a bit and also build confidence, something I did myself as a destroyer captain a decade later. On that occasion I had the entire wardroom crowd onto the back of the bridge in life jackets as the newly designated officer of the deck took the watch. The look on his face when he turned and saw us all decked out was priceless. We had a good laugh, congratulated him, and piled the big orange jackets by the bridge wing door on the way out.

Some very popular television shows have focused on servicemembers' use of humor to defuse difficult moments. Three particularly germane examples are *Hogan's Heroes*, about life in a German prisoner-of-war camp with the hopelessly stupid Sergeant Shultz and the constantly outwitted Colonel Klink; *McHale's Navy*, featuring a clever patrol boat skipper in World War II in the Pacific; and the best of all, *M.A.S.H.*, the story of personnel at a hospital operating at the extreme forward edge of combat operations in the Korean War. Such scenarios are hardly laughing matters, yet the episodes are full of humor. While the storylines are not realistic, the characters' constant joking around to ease their nerves in very difficult situations certainly is true to life in the military.

It is worth noting that there have been plenty of times when I failed to use humor well or at all. Particularly when I'm exhausted, it is hard to muster the requisite smile or ironic comment. Too often I have resorted to being sarcastic or sharp in pointing out someone else's failure. That isn't using humor to defuse the situation. Instead, it embarrasses the target and ends up adding tension. There is a fine distinction between humor and sarcasm, and at times I've missed the mark.

In *A Confederacy of Dunces*, we have a very funny novel with a tragicomic outcome. It is certainly not a novel that explores mainstream life. Indeed, I've never met anyone remotely like Ignatius Reilly. But it gives us the idea of using humor as a fundamental part of a life strategy to deal not only with deep adversity but also with the inherent absurdity that accompanies many human endeavors. From combat at sea around the world to the tense board rooms of New York and the staid classrooms of New England, I've tried to find the humor in every situation and deploy it as part of my leadership strategy. And I learned to do that by reading the story of Ignatius Reilly in *A Confederacy of Dunces*. He is certainly not a traditional hero, but this is a powerful and important American novel—and a damn funny one, too.

CHAPTER SIX

PREPARE DEEPLY FOR THE KEY EVENTS

Crusade in Europe

by Dwight David Eisenhower

If any blame or fault attaches to the attempt,
it is mine alone.

—Gen. Dwight Eisenhower prior to the D-Day invasion

In my library at home I have more than five thousand books. In subject matter they range across virtually every discipline of human knowledge—from history to science, literature, technology, art, exploration, maritime studies, and many others. As is true of most home libraries, there is a handful of books that have special meaning for me and have had a major impact on my life and career. These, of course, are the books I am discussing in *The Admiral's Bookshelf*.

I hold each of these books dear, but I put only one book at the very top of the list: Gen. Dwight Eisenhower's magisterial *Crusade in Europe*. I've read it cover-to-cover several times and often flip it open to refresh my memory on its broad strategic narrative or to remind myself of some important fact. I own three first editions of the book. One was presented to me by the enlisted men and women of my organization when I left command of NATO. The other two are rare signed copies of the first edition, first printing. Collectively, this trio is the very heart of my library.

There are four reasons *Crusade in Europe* appeals so deeply to me personally. Most important, General Eisenhower will always hold the honor of being the first Supreme Allied Commander of NATO. He took the job at the request of President Harry Truman and returned to Europe as the Cold War began to ramp up in serious and dangerous ways. Because I was the sixteenth in that line of four-star officers (Eisenhower was the only one to be a five-star General of the Army), his book has special resonance to me. When I was Supreme Allied Commander, I sat behind the desk where he once sat, and gazed across the room at the same globe that had graced that office then. It is only natural that the book fascinates me.

Second, the book means so much to me because of my deep respect for General Eisenhower as a leader. Virtually every page offers a significant example of how good leaders operate. Ike's innate modesty, his idea of "servant leadership" and taking care of the people in his command, and his good-natured sense of humor radiate from the pages, even after the eight decades that have passed since he was in command in Europe. I have studied and practiced leadership for much of my professional life, and I can say without doubt that the book is a master class in the subject, matched only by a couple of other important memoirs.

Third, *Crusade in Europe* is at heart a book of geopolitics. Dealing with the clash of great powers playing out across the vast European theater was an enormous challenge for Eisenhower. He had to understand and inculcate the history, culture, geography, military philosophy, and combat capability of many disparate foes and allies, holding the alliance together while seeking to divide and conquer its opponents. If you wish to understand the mechanisms of geopolitics, this is the book for you.

Lastly, the book is a study in interpersonal psychology. Ike's supreme gift (pun intended) was something commonly referred to today as "emotional intelligence." While he certainly possessed a temper and did not suffer fools, he had an unusual ability to encourage others to lean toward him, even in controversial moments. People simply liked Ike and often found themselves agreeing with him as a result. To be able to exercise that gift in the midst of a vast war among people as fundamentally different and famously difficult as the three powerful generals Bernard Montgomery, Charles de Gaulle, and George Patton was remarkable. Even less cantankerous officers like Omar Bradley and George Marshall (his boss, of course) fell under his charm. And those lists don't include some very querulous admirals, by the way.

Above all, the book has taught me to try to identify and prepare for the truly important events, the way Ike did for D-Day. Too often in our day-to-day lives we tend to let relatively unimportant events absorb our time and attention. We snap open our electronic in-boxes and spend hours answering questions and solving problems that in the big scheme of things won't have any significant impact. Ike could put the considerable power of his intellect, attention, and focus on the truly vital. And he made sure his team knew what those matters were and stayed in synch with him in executing his decisions.

Two examples from my own career illustrate how the book influenced my thinking. The first occurred during my time as commander of U.S. Southern Command. My top priority was to rescue three Americans being held hostage by FARC guerrillas deep in the jungles of Colombia. This meant that every day I received a significant briefing on the latest intelligence, coordinated with my special operations commander, and sought to keep the command focused on this vital objective. It would have been easy to let other important matters distract us from this seemingly intractable mission. But we eventually achieved their rescue with zero loss of life as part of a plan generated by our Colombian allies, fulfilling another key tenet of Ike's book—working hand-in-hand with our allies, partners, and friends.

The second example took place during my four-year tour at NATO. Here the central organizing task was the war in Afghanistan. During that period we had 150,000 troops from 50 nations engaged in the operation. A central part of our mission was to ensure that Afghanistan was able to hold elections. It was an incredibly difficult task that required the total focus of the entire vast NATO organization for success. Here again, I strove to keep the alliance focused on the vital mission at hand using many of the principles of Ike's book. The tragic ending of our efforts in Afghanistan a decade later saddened me immensely, especially when I thought back to the 2009–13 period when we were able to push the Taliban back into the mountains and facilitate democratic elections. In both cases, I shaped much of my command philosophy around the ideas I learned from *Crusade in Europe*.

There have also been plenty of points in my career when I failed to meet the standards of Ike's character, especially his superb sense of balance in command. When I held his old job as Supreme Allied Commander of NATO, I had two very difficult subordinates, both also four-star officers. One was an American, and the other was from an allied nation. The American had a chip on his shoulder from the time I arrived in the job and made my life difficult with a constant stream of criticisms flowing from his headquarters up to mine. Rather than rise above his attitude and take it in stride, as Ike would have done, I tended to either ignore him or brusquely override his advice. I didn't do a good job trying to co-opt his considerable talents and harness them for the team. In the case of the allied four-star, the problem there was his inability to accept thoughtful comments from his political bosses back home. It made him a frequent liability, and I never managed to find a way to smooth his political path back in his nation's capital. Ike would have done better in both scenarios, I suspect.

Ike's book is structured chronologically from the very start of World War II in 1939 and continues crisply and succinctly to the end of the war in Europe in 1945. It is beautifully illustrated with dozens of maps, charts, and black-and-white photographs that help readers follow the narrative. Because it is written in the first person, readers feel the weight of the big decisions Ike made as well as his day-to-day frustrations with both bureaucracy and logistics. The civilian politics of the day, from Washington to London to Moscow, are integrated into the discussions and give a shape and feel to the narrative that is both personal and geopolitical.

There are certainly flaws in the book, as there are in any history that is told from a singular point of view. Ike sought to avoid ruffling feathers unnecessarily and tended to smooth over the rough edges of relationships that other multi-viewpoint histories indicate were very frustrating for him—notably with the British general Bernard Montgomery, whose insistence on caution Ike sometimes found maddening.

Historians can also debate some of General Eisenhower's judgments in the book. He tends to understate the contributions and successes of the Russians, including the wartime record of Field Marshal Georgy Zhukov, the best of the Soviet combat leaders. This can be attributed to the emerging tensions between the United States and the Soviet Union during the period when Ike was drafting the book, which was published three years after the end of the war in 1948. Equally understandable given the tenor of the times is Ike's frequently stated scorn for Germany's warfighting prowess and refusal to give fair credit to some of the German field successes. Finally, Ike's skepticism, bordering on disdain, for Gen. George Patton—a frequently aggravating subordinate who provided him with both successes and failures, both on the battlefield and in the realm of public affairs—is palpable.

As the book opens in late 1941, the future Supreme Allied Commander and five-star General of the Army Dwight Eisenhower is a lowly one-star brigadier general assigned to the Army's war plans division. Marshall spots Ike's abilities, and he is elevated quickly, reaching three-star rank by mid-year 1942.

At this point, Ike's vantage point shifts to an underground headquarters on Gibraltar, where he is entrusted with planning and executing Operation Torch, the vital North Africa campaign. Given the French connections with North Africa, this marks the beginning of Eisenhower's need to deal with the vicious rivalries and difficult personalities he will face over the coming years. Operation Torch suffered frustrating losses at the Kasserine Pass but ultimately resulted in victory and the invasion of Sicily. Montgomery figures prominently, and managing the mercurial Brit becomes one of Ike's principal challenges.

The heart of the book, of course, centers on Operational Overlord, the Allies' invasion of France. President Roosevelt personally chose Ike to command the mission as Supreme Allied Commander of the Allied Expeditionary Force, selecting him above Gen. George Marshall, his boss. As the invasion was about to get under way, Ike famously prepared two statements to announce the operation to the public: one in the case of victory (a characteristically modest announcement giving credit to others) and the other in the case of defeat (in which he took full responsibility for the failure). Of the many lessons I have taken from the book, this is the one that has always stuck with me. It is worth reading from time to time Ike's statement of defeat, which, of course, was never used:

> Our landings in the Cherbourg-Havre area have failed to gain a satisfactory foothold and I have withdrawn the troops. My decision to attack at this time and place was based on the best information available. The troops, the air and the Navy did all that bravery and devotion to duty could do. If any blame or fault attaches to the attempt, it is mine alone.

> **"If any blame or fault attaches to the attempt, it is mine alone."**

The book continues with the intense combat campaigns that followed the invasion on June 6, 1944, until the final German surrender on May 8, 1945. Along the way, Ike was promoted to General of the Army, becoming one of a tiny handful of five-star generals in U.S. history. The most dangerous point in the narrative occurs in December 1944, when the Nazis staged a determined counterattack in the Ardennes that became known as the Battle of the Bulge.

Ike's descriptions of that battle, which required significant shifts on the battlefield, is in itself a masterful description of how strategists must be capable of changing their plan quickly and efficiently. Ike, a brilliant planner, later said, "the plan is nothing, but planning is everything." He meant that the entire process of planning—assembling the team, analyzing the situation, determining the courses of action, ensuring resources and logistics are present—is what matters. Plans are always subject to decisions made by the enemy, and no plan survives first contact with them. The essential lesson is that if you have developed a detailed plan that allows multiple options, you can always change the plan in the middle of the action—as Ike did in concert with his generals in the desperate hours of the Battle of the Bulge.

Throughout the book we see the wisdom in Churchill's adage that the only thing worse than fighting alongside allies—with the constant bickering, disagreements, and shifting objectives that entails—is to try and fight *without* allies. Ike believed that to his core, and in the book he summarizes that point perfectly in prose that is worth repeating:

> The democracies must learn that the world is now too small for the rigid concepts of national sovereignty that developed in a time when the nations were self-sufficient and self-dependent for their own wellbeing and safety. None of them today can stand alone. No radical surrender of national sovereignty is required—only a firm agreement that in disputes between nations a central and joint agency, after examination of the facts, shall decide the justice of the case by majority vote and thereafter shall have the power and the means to enforce its decision. This is a slight restriction indeed on nationalism and a small price to pay if thereby the peoples who stand for human liberty are better fitted to settle dissension within their own ranks or to meet attack from without.

Chapter Six

Prepare deeply for the key events. Work with allies, partners, and friends. Be thoughtful and low key with all those you meet. Be prepared to change the plan. Take responsibility when things go wrong and share credit when you succeed. These simple adages all resonate deeply with me and have helped me again and again in my voyage. Every time I pick up Ike's book, I smile and think of my far more distinguished predecessor, and silently thank him for writing this extraordinary volume.

The book's title comes from a speech Ike made on the eve of the D-Day invasion, in which he said, "Soldiers, Sailors and Airmen of the Allied Expeditionary Force! You are about to embark upon the Great Crusade, toward which we have striven these many months. The eyes of the world are upon you." To read *Crusade in Europe* even today, at this great distance, is to dive deeply into a moment in history when one of the remarkable leaders of the twentieth century wrestled with astounding challenges—and surmounted them.

CHAPTER SEVEN

STAY PHYSICALLY FIT

The Boys in the Boat
by Daniel Brown

Rowing then becomes a kind of perfect language.
Poetry, that's what a good swing feels like.

I can remember hitting a moment of complete exhaustion as a sea captain in command of USS *Barry* in 1994. We had been conducting high-paced operations off the coast of Serbia, participating in a blockade to prevent weapons from flowing into the hands of the cruel and oppressive Serbian regime that was committing genocide on its Croatian and Bosnian neighbors in the awful Balkan Wars of the early 1990s.

We were operating very close to the coast, trying to interdict small coastal trawlers seeking to smuggle in weapons, and I had to be on the bridge every minute. The navigation margin was tight, and the tactical decisions—intercept, fire warning shots, send a boarding team—were essentially instantaneous. So, I simply stayed awake, drank pot after pot of coffee, and tried to keep my eyes open and my brain engaged. I figured our time on the line was "only" ten days and I could tough it out until we concluded. We had a port visit to Corfu, Greece, scheduled next, and I planned to sleep then.

Perhaps I could have made it through given my relative youth—I was only thirty-seven at the time—and my decent state of fitness; but just as we finished up our period of duty on the blockade line, fate intervened. Saddam Hussein was making another attempt to invade Kuwait, and the carrier USS *George Washington*—the centerpiece of our carrier battle group—was detached to proceed at flank speed out of the Mediterranean, through the Suez Canal, down the Red Sea, and into the waters of the Arabian Gulf to deter him. *Barry* was selected as the carrier's escort.

We sprinted across the eastern Med, refueled from the carrier at sea at extremely high speed, and entered the Suez Canal—all evolutions that required the presence of the captain on the bridge. By that point I literally was dozing off in my captain's chair on the right side of the bridge and had given the officer of the deck instructions to wake me every ten minutes or so. I had almost nothing left in the tank.

We were sailing southbound in the Suez Canal and, as is customary, pulled out of the main channel to anchor and let a northbound convoy go by. The "parking lot" in the canal is a flat body of water appropriately called the Great Bitter Lake. We had an Egyptian pilot embarked, a former Egyptian naval officer, whose job was to give us specific directions about where to anchor our big destroyer. He did not inspire a great deal of confidence, but I was so exhausted I simply acquiesced in his directions. We were headed toward the anchorage he had designated for us when my navigator, a very young lieutenant named Robb Chadwick, said with real urgency in his voice, "Captain, we are standing into danger. Our charts show shallows ahead. Recommend all stop and anchor here."

I conveyed this to the pilot, who insisted we continue to the anchorage he had designated. My exhaustion level was such that I couldn't summon the energy to do anything but continue along. My circuits were simply fried. Fortunately, young Lieutenant Chadwick took the virtually unimaginable step of overruling me, taking the conn of the ship, bringing us to all stop, and dropping the anchor. The Egyptian pilot was outraged. Robb's actions shook me out of my stupor, and I ordered a small boat launched to sound the water ahead with an old-fashioned lead line to physically measure the depth.

Sure enough, the anchorage where the pilot had been directing us was too shallow for *Barry*'s deep draft; had we proceeded, we would have run aground. A naval officer who runs their ship aground almost always sees their career quickly terminated. The embarrassed pilot sulked for the rest of the transit. I told the young lieutenant (who is now a rear admiral, by the way) he had done the right thing, turned the deck over to my second in command, and went below to sleep. My executive officer, a lieutenant commander, whispered in my ear as I went below, "Right call, Cap'n. Don't forget, sleep is a weapon too."

I've thought about that moment many times over the years, turning over in my mind the importance of balancing activity with rest in command. Allowing myself to become so totally exhausted was a complete failure on my part. I went on to have a half-dozen commands after *Barry*, and I think I managed to keep that sleeping/waking blend reasonably well structured. As I think about how to best keep that balance, I am always struck by the importance of physical fitness in allowing each of us to perform at peak and ensure we do not hit a moment of debilitating exhaustion as I did in the Suez Canal.

Which brings us to *The Boys in the Boat*. There are hundreds of books about athletes honing their ability to perform at their peak—literally dozens about every sport. But the best one I've ever read is Dan Brown's extraordinary portrait of the University of Washington crew team as they prepared for—and ultimately won—the 1936 Olympics.

The story is deceptively simple. An eight-man rowing team from the state of Washington, young men from lower-middle-class backgrounds, managed to defeat the teams from East Coast rowing giants Harvard and Yale to get to the Olympics, and then narrowly defeated Germany and Italy to win the Olympic gold medal. Hitler himself was in the audience, and the emerging Nazi empire was absolutely determined to prevail—indeed, this was much more a geopolitical competition than an athletic one. Brown's description of the final race is both heart-stopping and exhilarating. While none of the team's members went on to lead a significant individual public life, all of them remained in touch throughout their lives and came together year after year to go on the water together and row.

Several things make this a remarkable and unique book. First is the sport itself: crew. No other sport has the simultaneous demands of deep cardiovascular exertion alongside brute strength requirements on the entire body *and* simultaneously requires fine motor skill management of an unwieldy oar dipping repetitively in and out of unforgiving water.

During my time at the Naval Academy, I played both varsity tennis and squash, which imposed their own kind of demands, but I was in awe of the effort required of the crew teams. I would not have lasted a week on the team, even as the coxswain, the only position I might have aspired to conquer. The sport simply demands more of the participant's body than any other, including lengthy twice-a-day workouts. The portrait Brown sketches of the training regime confirms this; the grinding pain of the exercise is almost palpable to readers.

Second, in addition to the enormous demands on the body, crew is a deeply mental sport. It pushes the rower to efforts beyond where the human body ought to operate. This is certainly true of other sports as well, notably long-distance running, boxing, and wrestling, but the need to simply override the screaming pain imposed on the rower's body in a crew shell is remarkable. In *The Boys in the Boat*, the ability of the team's coach to manage the mental side of the young men's training regime, intercollegiate competitions, and ultimately the Olympics is a study in mind over matter. The coach tells the team, "Men as fit as you, when your everyday strength is gone, can draw on a mysterious reservoir of power far greater. Then it is that you can reach for the stars. That is the way champions are made."

Third, in the book we see the beneficial aspects of not only pure physical training—weight lifting, sprinting, long-distance runs—but also the importance of balanced nutrition, sufficient sleep, avoiding toxic substances, and mental preparation. During my naval career I had individuals on my team who were extraordinary physical specimens—SEALs and Green Berets who had surmounted arduous physical training regimes—but failed to reach peak performance because they neglected the nonphysical aspects of their fitness. In *The Boys in the Boat*, we see an enlightened coach who knows how to put all the aspects of human preparation—both physical and mental—together effectively.

Finally, the book aptly demonstrates the connections of teamwork that make crew so special. Many sports require teamwork, of course. Even on a tennis or squash team, where the competition is individual, the overall score is additive, and teammates work together and cheer each other on. But in a rowing shell, the eight oarsmen must literally meld their motions, duplicating each other's movements precisely, in order to achieve the overall desired outcome of high-speed propulsion. The book describes how the boys were able to find their rhythm, overcome differences in their backgrounds and physical skills, and ultimately achieve a remarkable level of teamwork.

> "Every man in the boat had absolute confidence in every one of his mates. Why they won cannot be attributed to individuals. Heartfelt cooperation all spring was responsible for the victory."

I have been reminded again and again that there is a direct correlation between physical fitness and all aspects of human performance. Even in my thirties, at the peak of my physical abilities, I worked hard to remain physically fit. One reason for doing so was a continuing enjoyment of racket sports, which I still play with enthusiasm today. Another reason back then was that I wanted the physical stamina to keep up with my young daughters. And I found that in periods when I slacked off on my physical training, I paid the price in two ways. First, it was progressively harder to get back into shape each time I slacked off, picked up some pounds, and stopped working out hard. Second, there was an immediate and very real drop in my level of energy and attention to the day-to-day challenges of my job.

But a crucial reason for maintaining physical fitness was the key lesson I learned in *The Boys in the Boat*: the more you put into physical training and overall fitness, the better your total performance will be. And the countervailing lesson is equally profound: if you neglect fitness, you will pay a price in performance. That can be a ship run aground in the Great Bitter Lake, a ruined career, or a failed military mission. It can also be faulty judgments in analysis at your desk working for a multinational corporation or, worst of all, failings in your personal life as exhaustion and weakness lead to wrecked relationships.

Finally, a concluding grace note about this fine book. Beyond the lessons it imparts so effectively about fitness, it is also a lovely portrait of a very different United States of America. To pick up and read *The Boys in the Boat* is to return to a time nearly a century ago when Americans did a better job of finding balance in their daily lives, long before the Internet and smartphones dragged us apart. It is a book about who we once were: instinctively hardworking, uniformly patriotic, unified in taking on important missions, and generally possessed of a healthy sense of humor and perspective.

I dip into this book from time to time to remind myself of the vital importance of physical and mental fitness, but also to visit—just for a moment—a different earlier version of our nation. There is much to admire in the portrait of our nation that emerges in *The Boys in the Boat*. Let's hope we have the strength to find our way back.

CHAPTER EIGHT

SEEK TO INNOVATE

Steve Jobs

by Walter Isaacson

Innovation distinguishes between a
leader and a follower.

Biographies are hit or miss for me. So often I pick up a highly touted biography and am disappointed to find myself buried immediately in mundane details of no interest to me. I really don't care about genealogy going back several generations, nor am I interested in learning what the person had for breakfast when they were growing up. Too many biographies simply march along describing the subject's ordinary day-to-day life.

But an occasional biography really sings for me, generally when the biographer manages to do two things very well. The first is simple to say but hard to do: bring the principal to life.

Make the protagonist of the biography a very real person, with all the faults and virtues they exhibited in their presumably fascinating life. Here I want to know everything from the tone of their voice to the temper of their passions. Are they interesting? Would I want to have cocktails with them or a long dinner? Who did they love and who did they hate? What are or were they *really* like?

The second thing, and even more important in creating an effective biography, is to provide a portrait of the person's times. What was happening in the world around them, and how did they not only fit into the period but contribute to shaping it? This is biography becoming, in effect, applied history, sketching how the life of this man or woman collided with an important moment in human history. The best books of this genre answer that fundamental question: What was the subject's role in the important events of the time?

There are plenty of fine biographies out there, and I've read a handful that accomplish both of those admittedly difficult charges. When I finished, I almost felt that I had literally met the subject, and I had a sense of how the person's life fit into and shaped a crucial time. They were teaching texts. Thus, the very best biographies can help readers shape our own journey by taking what we admire in that person and then trying—often in far smaller but still important ways—to apply it in a useful manner.

In the world of the military, reading a powerful biography—say, of a World War II admiral like Chester Nimitz—can inspire younger officers and help guide the trajectories of their own leadership voyages. Two extraordinary naval biographers I can cite in that regard are E. B. Potter and Thomas Buell. Between them, they wrote biographies of not only Admiral Nimitz but also his World War II contemporaries the admirals Arleigh Burke, Ernest King, and Raymond Spruance. Of the four admirals, the only one

I met personally was Arleigh Burke, and he was in his nineties at the time. But through those fine biographies I feel I knew those officers in their prime, and I have felt their influence in how I approached many decisions in my own naval career.

Arguably the very best biographer plying his craft today is the affable and thoughtful journalist Walter Isaacson, former editor of *Time* magazine and CEO of CNN. I've come to know Walter over the past couple of decades, and we served briefly together on the board of the Rockefeller Foundation. As an author, he has created a series of stunningly vivid portraits of historical innovators. Taken together, these biographies are a master class on what it means to be a disrupter of society, technology, and culture. His subjects include Leonardo da Vinci, Benjamin Franklin, Albert Einstein, and—most recently—Elon Musk. But his best portrait, in my view, is that of the complex and brilliant founder of Apple, Steven Jobs, published in 2001, the same year Jobs died of pancreatic cancer.

I will admit a particular affinity for Steven Jobs, as we are very close in age, born ten days apart in 1955. He was born in California and adopted almost immediately after his birth. In his early years Jobs had difficulty in traditional educational settings and used drugs, notably LSD. He attended the fascinating and eclectic Reed College briefly, and in 1976—the year a very straitlaced Jim Stavridis was graduating from Annapolis—founded Apple with Steve Wozniak. He was among the first to see the power of smaller, hipper, cooler personal computers, and he experienced both failures (Lisa) and successes (Macintosh). His career had extraordinary ups and downs and dramatic twists and turns, including leaving Apple in 1985 and then returning in 1997. A big difference between us, I should note, is simple and irrefutable: Steve Jobs was a genius, and I am not. Plus, he was a lot taller and had great hair.

His bent for innovation and his marketing genius led to a wide variety of products that are integral to our lives today—iMac, iPod, iTunes, iPhone, as well as an entire commercial support structure to propagate them: App Store, Apple Store, and iTunes Store. Jobs focused his genius on both hardware and software and was obsessive in his concern for how every aspect of Apple products should look and feel for the consumer. His devotion to work was legendary. Even after he was diagnosed with pancreatic cancer in 2003, he still managed to impact Apple until his death in 2011 at the age of fifty-six. I followed his career avidly, both for the superb products—which I continue to use today—and also for two aspects of his life and career that have deeply influenced mine and are worthy of emulation.

The first is prosaic, but it has served me well and I commend it to anyone: Steve Jobs had the ability to build a truly effective presentation to convince an audience that his product was the best of the best. His presentations used very simple, oversized images rather than the complicated, wordy, overdetailed Power-Points too many presenters use. His ability to put up a big image and simply talk the audience through what it meant was iconic.

> **"Simplicity, that is the ultimate sophistication."**

I adopted that simple style for my own use, dumping my old wordy, Pentagon-style presentations and gradually simplifying them to single images that captured what I wanted to say. When I briefed the NATO Council and the heads of the twenty-eight nations at a summit on Afghanistan, I didn't use forty slides crammed with verbiage about trends and difficulties and the challenges we faced; I showed a simple photograph of young girls walking down a mountain road toward a school we had built.

With that photo as the focus, I discussed the successes and failures of the campaign. For years I was an over-wordy, bogged-down-in-detail kind of Pentagon briefer—until I learned from Steve Jobs to be better.

People remember the big images long after they've forgotten the details. A year later, President Obama told me at a White House dinner that he couldn't forget the image I showed of the young women going to school with the mountains in the background. Simple, powerful images stay with people and make enduring points. I learned that from Steve Jobs and have used that style of presentation since.

But the much more important thing I learned from Steve Jobs, primarily through reading this remarkable biography, was the power and need for innovation. While Walter Isaacson was crafting the book, he conducted more than forty interviews with Jobs, and hundreds of others with family members, friends, competitors, adversaries, and observers. And the critical messages he took from these conversations were about innovation—about disruption and changing the world. As Steve Jobs famously said, "We're here to put a dent in the universe. Otherwise, why else even be here?"

As I was reading the book I found ideas about innovation that became core to my own approach—first as a senior military commander and later as dean of a graduate school of international relations, and today as vice chairman for global affairs at a large international financial firm. From this fine biography I have taken away three key points on innovation.

First, it must begin at the top. Those at the top of the organization come up with some of the new ideas, but they also—and more importantly—create the conditions that allow innovation to flourish in the organization. Leaders must let those in their organizations know that they are always looking for new ideas.

At U.S. Southern Command, for example, one of my key missions was anti-narcotics interdictions.

We learned that the Colombian drug lords were out-innovating us by building high-tech mini-submarines to move dope through the Caribbean. After we caught one such submarine, I had the team mount it on a pedestal in front of our headquarters in Doral, Florida. I wanted everyone on my team to know what we were up against, that we valued innovation, and that our competitors valued it as well. Twentieth-century competition, in the end, is brain-on-brain warfare.

A second crucial lesson is that leaders must provide space and resources to the innovators. While you can very seldom, if ever, run an organization driving for change and innovation every second, you can very effectively apportion an appropriate level of command resources (money, time, training opportunities). This can be as little as 5–10 percent of the organization's total resources or as much as 50–70 percent depending on the type of organization and the resources involved. When I became dean of the Fletcher School at Tufts University, a top graduate school of international relations, about a decade ago, two things quickly became clear to me. First, we needed to innovate in how we delivered education; for example, well before the pandemic we were working to achieve a new emphasis on online courses. Our efforts to build a credible online program paid off enormously when the lockdowns began and helped the school thrive through that very difficult period. Setting up the online capabilities was not a huge investment—perhaps 10 percent of our budget—but it turned out to be a very successful innovation.

Second, and more complex and difficult to implement, we had to revise the graduate school curriculum. We had remained too focused on highly traditional aspects of diplomacy and international relations and neglected to develop courses and majors reflecting new trends. Changing this was very hard, because professors love to teach what they have always taught, and many were guarded by tenure from being forced to change.

But by putting to use a significant chunk of resources (again, money, time, and in this case opportunity to teach new subjects) we managed to wrench the curriculum into the twenty-first century. The new courses included graduate work on the role of gender in international relations, the Arctic, the growing importance of India, and the impact of climate and the environment on world affairs. Perhaps most important, we created an entirely new degree in cybersecurity, partnering with the fine computer science department at Tufts (shades of Steve Jobs). All of this was expensive—requiring more than 30 percent of our budget for several years—and culturally difficult. Had I not had the model of Steve Jobs in front of me, it would have been much harder to think it all through and ultimately execute it.

Finally, studying and learning about Steve Jobs was a lesson in business and marketing innovation. In my job today, I am deeply involved in the world of international finance, credit markets, and decisions about investments globally. In essence, I am the chief geopolitical officer of my firm, and I have to answer the "so what" question from my partners when I describe events in Russia, Ukraine, China, Iran, North Korea, and other international hotspots. Learning about the life of Jobs—the crazy ups and downs in his business trajectory and both his successes and failures in innovation—made me much more capable of interacting credibly with business leaders and investors around the world. Business innovators can learn a great deal from Jobs' successes and his failures.

When I look back on my career, I can produce a simple graph of innovation versus accomplishment. In the jobs where I was timid or conservative in my approach, I never got the kind of impressive results I hoped for. As I learned to be less afraid and to try new ideas, my performance improved. The more I innovated, the better I did, and the converse was true as well. Perhaps the job where I had the most impact overall was leading the Navy innovation and tactical warfare think tank, Deep Blue, in the immediate days and months after 9/11. As a ship captain on USS *Barry*, on the other hand, I was too conservative and afraid of failing to try big new ideas. Steve Jobs never doubted that he wanted always to seize the big new idea. I wish I could look back at my own career and say the same.

Steve Jobs is a short and simply named biography of a remarkable and unique American by a preeminent historian, Walter Isaacson. But the relatively brief and utterly complex life story of Steve Jobs offers many, many lessons—especially about innovation.

CHAPTER NINE

WORK SMART

Flashman

by George MacDonald Fraser

Courage—and shuffle the cards.

I am not a scoundrel. I've tried to live up to the ideals of my family and the U.S. Navy throughout my life, always seeking to exhibit courage, honor, and commitment. I believe in what I was taught on day one at the U.S. Naval Academy: an honorable person does not lie, cheat, or steal.

But among the guilty pleasures in my life are the brilliant novels of historical fiction by George MacDonald Fraser about a scoundrel: the irascible, cowardly, lecherous nineteenth-century British soldier Harry Flashman. And believe it or not, there is quite a bit of leadership (and some stunningly real battlefield descriptions) in the dozen novels of the very popular series published between 1969 and 2005.

A proud Scot, George MacDonald Fraser fought bravely in the Burma theater in World War II as a very young soldier and later wrote a marvelous memoir of his service, *Quartered Safe out Here* (stealing a line from Kipling's classic poem "Gunga Din"). He went on to become a journalist and professional writer, publishing his breakout novel, *Flashman*, in 1969.

The central protagonist was lifted from the pages of the classic nineteenth-century novel *Tom Brown's School Days*, where Harry Flashman appears as a drunken bully who is thrown out of his elite boarding school. The first novel of the series, *Flashman*, covers Flashman's backstory. He is forced to return home to his wealthy family after being expelled from boarding school and immediately tries to bed his father's paramour, without success.

Flashman is an impressive figure: athletic, handsome, and at six-foot-two quite tall for his time. He becomes determined to obtain a commission in the Army but makes his decision about which unit to join based on the cut of their uniform and the unlikelihood of their being sent into actual combat. From that unimpressive start he goes on to a remarkable career, ending up as General Sir Harry Paget Flashman, with an alphabet soup of British honors: VC, KCB, and KCIE.

As we come to know Flashman, we discover he is not only a physical and moral coward. He cheats at games of chance and is a skirt-chaser extraordinaire and a spendthrift. His only real skills are a facility to quickly learn languages (this is a plot device that Fraser makes use of time and again in the books), a true gift as a cavalryman with a superb touch with horses, and a bluff way of ingratiating himself with his seniors.

The books follow Flashman's life and career through a series of incredible adventures, including service in various important British military campaigns in India, Afghanistan, and the

Crimean War. He also has liaison duties in the American Civil War, on the China front, in Africa, and in the Native American wars in America (including surviving the Battle of Little Big Horn). He is present (and generally trying to avoid danger) at the charge of the Light Brigade in Crimea, the sieges of Cawnpore and Lucknow in the Sepoy Mutiny in India, the Taiping Rebellion in China, John Brown's raid on Harper's Ferry, and the Siege of Khartoum. Flashman is a cad, a rake, a drunk, a liar, a cheater, and a braggart; in sum, he is a scoundrel.

I could have chosen any of the dozen Flashman novels to add to *The Admiral's Bookshelf*, but the first one best captures the essence of the man. In *Flashman*, our antihero manages to join the famous 11th Regiment of Light Dragoons commanded by Lord Cardigan. Flashman is disciplined over a love affair by being posted to Scotland for a cooling-off period. He is forced into marriage after seducing a wealthy Scotsman's daughter, and Lord Cardigan throws him out of the regiment.

These unfortunate events lead to Flashman being sent to a humble position in the East India Company in British India. While there, he is sent on an expedition to Afghanistan, where he witnesses the disastrous retreat from Kabul in 1842 and the massacre of thousands of British and colonial troops and camp followers by the Afghans in one of the worst defeats in British military history. He is present at the siege of Jalalabad and the final stand at Gandamak, both enormously important battles in the history of the British army.

> "We stood there for a full half hour, like so many scarecrows, while they jeered at us from a distance, and one or two of us were shot down."

Why highlight a book about such an unreformed bounder? Surely there is nothing to admire or learn from Flashman. Or is there?

First of all, I commend the books generally to anyone seeking to understand the history of the British Empire in the nineteenth century. They take the reader quite accurately behind the scenes of the British forces, but also inside the councils of their opponents. Through these novels, readers see the British colonial and great power conflicts from the other side of the table. Flashman has a way of ending up in close contact with Britain's opponents, and the portraits Fraser paints of Russians, Afghans, rebellious Indians and Chinese, and anticolonial forces generally are vivid and meticulously researched. The battle sequences are likewise excellent and realistic, from the cavalry charges in the Crimean War to Custer's last stand.

Aside from their historical accuracy the novels are also well written and incredibly entertaining. They present a master class in how an author pulls together a story, creates fascinating characters, and—above all—manages to put unexpected and unreliable characters like Harry Flashman on center stage. *Flashman* provides indelible portraits not only of Flashman himself but also of the incredible group of British and Afghan characters he meets. Of note, we see firsthand the (arguably) worst general in British history, Major-General William Elphinstone, whose hapless command led to the deaths of nearly twenty thousand British troops, their families, and camp follower civilians in 1842 when they retreated from Kabul.

More importantly, the novels show us a main character who lacks scruples and a moral compass but is a highly intelligent actor within his slightly bent set of objectives. Harry Flashman "works smart," meaning he is constantly seeking a clever way out of the challenges his own ambitions create for him. If there is a better horse available, he will find it and appropriate it. No one is better than Flashman at attracting brave, capable, and loyal subordinates who will protect him. Again and again Flashman finds servants, sergeants, and junior officers who become part of the team of minders surrounding him (and for many of them, it doesn't turn out well). He also is able to spot new technologies on the battlefield and is unafraid to put them to use, from advanced firearms to better maps and charts. Flashman always seems to find a shortcut across the battlefield and can camouflage himself with alacrity. His knowledge of numerous languages allows him to gain intelligence, understand the enemy, and escape from the proverbial sticky wickets. In short, he is someone who works smart.

While I've always eschewed the flawed moral posture of Flashman, I've tried to work smart in my own career as well. Employing new technologies is a good example. In counter-narcotics operations in Latin America when I served as commander of U.S. Southern Command, we used advanced radar and infrared devices to find drug-runners. In Afghanistan (ironically, the setting of *Flashman*) we devised new ways of finding and defending against the improvised explosive devices that were killing hundreds of our soldiers every month. We developed better armor, used satellites to detect newly dug patches on the roadways, and found ways to deflect blasts.

Like Harry Flashman, I love to study and learn languages, and that has often helped me in my various jobs. In the conference rooms and decision-making counsels of NATO, I often used both French (the second official language of the alliance) and Spanish in discussions with allies. Especially in Latin America, I was able to use Spanish, which I speak well, and Portuguese, which I continue to study, to work smart. To know another language is to have a window into someone else's ideas and beliefs.

I've often fallen short in using innovation, by the way. Too often, I've taken command and simply "stood the watch" without trying to find the right shortcuts and hacks that might have made a difference. Part of that is my own conservative nature, and part of it is how difficult it is for a commander to overcome the resistance of the staff. Admirals are taught an ironic riddle: "What do you call a series of Navy captains on the admiral's staff?" Answer: "A circuit of infinite impedance." A better admiral than I am would have been cleverer in overcoming the ingrained resistance I faced. Harry Flashman certainly would have tried, and probably succeeded.

Finally, I think of *Flashman* as a brilliant guide to the history and culture of Afghanistan. The portraits of the Afghan leaders that Fraser sketches mirror the faces I saw again and again in my four-year command of the NATO mission, the International Security Assistance Force-Afghanistan (ISAF). Because I had read about the actions of the Afghan leadership in the nineteenth century, I was able to command the 150,000 members of ISAF more effectively. *Flashman* was immensely helpful as well in dealing with Afghan allied leaders, including both Hamid Karzai and Ashraf Ghani. The book also heightened my ability to work with the NATO generals working for me in-country (Stan McChrystal, Dave Petraeus, John Allen, and Joe Dunford) in analyzing appropriate courses of action. Above all, it helped us get into the minds of the Afghan Taliban and understand something of their history and cultural mindset. That too was working smart.

Sometimes, the great lessons of literature show us how *not* to behave. Certainly, Harry Flashman's deeply flawed character is an example of exactly who we do not want to become in terms of his moral compass. He distinctly does not sail true north. But as a smart, savvy, canny innovator in a host of dangerous situations,

Flashman shows us how to intelligently use all the tools at our disposal to reverse our fortunes and survive to fight another day. That's working smart, and Harry Flashman shows us how to do it again and again.

CHAPTER TEN

THINK INDEPENDENTLY

The Handmaid's Tale

by Margaret Atwood

A rat in a maze is free to go anywhere, as long
as it stays inside the maze.

—Offred, a Handmaid in Gilead

Among the most chilling dystopian novels ever written, *The Handmaid's Tale* is a masterpiece by one of our greatest living writers. Dame Margaret Atwood is a two-time Booker Prize recipient (the highest award in writing, save only for the Nobel Prize in Literature). I met her once in Canada by the grace of the Canadian chief of defense, General Walt Natynczyk, who knew I was an enormous admirer of her work.

Atwood has piercing eyes, a friendly manner, and a penetrating wit. In our brief conversation we spoke about everything from the genesis of *The Handmaid's Tale* (certainly her best-known work) to contemporary U.S. politics (she is not a fan). She graciously autographed several of her works that I particularly admire, and which I treasure in my library today. Now that American Cormac McCarthy (my other favorite author) has passed on, Dame Margaret is at the top of my wish list to win the Nobel.

The Handmaid's Tale is a difficult book to read because the subject matter is so brutally distasteful. Published in 1985, it describes a near-future period in which the United States is controlled by a totalitarian government led by patriarchal white supremacists. In the Republic of Gilead, men are utterly dominant over women, controlling every aspect of their lives.

Atwood opens the book with a brief history of how the United States lost its democracy in a revolution launched by the "Sons of Jacob," who suspended the Constitution and instituted a biblically inspired society founded on the principles of the Old Testament. Women cannot read, write, own property, or hold money, and they cannot be in public unaccompanied. Radiation and pollution have rendered most of the women in Gilead infertile, and thus a subclass is created, the Handmaids, fertile young women who are forced to produce children for the ruling class. Women are separated into various castes and wear identifying colors. The Commanders' Wives wear light blue; the Handmaids red; widows black; and the Aunts, who train and rule the Handmaids, wear brown.

> "We thought we had such problems. How were we to know we were happy?"

Offred, a Handmaid who is on her third round of servicing a Commander and his Wife as a potential surrogate mother, is the protagonist. We never learn her name. She is called Offred after her Commander (she is "of Fred"). In flashbacks we see how Offred went in a single day from a well-educated, financially independent woman to a virtual slave. We learn of her failed attempts to escape, the loss of her husband and daughter, and the sheer brutality of her indoctrination as a Handmaid. Her life is restricted to her room in the Commander's house, a room downstairs where she sits with the Commander's Wife, and daily walks paired with another Handmaid, always under the eyes of the Guardians. An elaborate sexual ritual intended only for procreation governs her contacts with the Commander. Despite strict rules against it, however, Offred's Commander takes her outside the house to a "social club" that is in fact a brothel for the elite males.

Offred begins a secret and highly dangerous affair with Nick, the Commander's chauffeur, and learns that there is an underground resistance network. When the affair is discovered, Offred is taken into custody by the Eyes of God, the secret police of Gilead. As she is taken from the Commander's house, certain she is about to die, Nick murmurs to her the resistance code word "Mayday" and "Trust me." Is she being rescued by the resistance or taken to prison and certain death?

This ambiguous ending is further amplified by an epilogue that includes a description of the events in the novel as having been recorded on tapes discovered by historians in Canada, which was not a part of Gilead. Indeed, in *The Testaments*, a sequel to *The Handmaid's Tale*, much of the story line is moved fifteen years into the future, and it is strongly implied that Offred did in fact escape Gilead and was reunited with her daughters.

The book is a chilling examination of authoritarian rule and the horror of a world in which women are powerless, have no control over their reproductive process, and are essentially chattel passed around by men. It examines how total control affects morality and the ways rules can be corrupted for the benefit of the powerful few. It likewise demonstrates the need for resistance to orthodoxy, the necessity of friendship to deal with adversity, and the power that derives from the willingness to take immense risks to overcome seemingly overwhelming odds.

But above all, to me the central message of *The Handmaid's Tale*, and the reason I include it in *The Admiral's Bookshelf*, is its advocacy for independent thinking. It is so often comfortable and easy to go along with the commonplace tropes in our day-to-day life, whether or not we actually believe them. Thinking in opposition to the conventional view is painful, often leads to failure and even to despair, and can be very dangerous to careers and even lives. But many of the greatest achievements in human history began with someone's willingness to challenge the orthodoxy of supposedly sacrosanct principles, from Galileo to Newton to Einstein in the world of science, for example.

The courage to think independently is perhaps even more important in the political realm. When people are willing to simply accept the control that a ruling regime holds over them, they lose their individual independence. Very few have the moral, intellectual, and at times the physical courage to challenge a dominant class structure.

If we return to the earliest days of the United States and our own Revolution, it is worth remembering that only about a third of the population actively supported independence. The other two-thirds were either enthusiastic about remaining a British colony (the status quo) or were neutral on the proposition. For the latter group, the risks probably felt out of proportion to the benefits; but, fortunately for our national future, there were strong supporters of independence from English rule. Those patriots, whose names are inscribed in the Declaration of Independence, knew well the risks—to reputation, property, and body—but were willing to challenge the orthodox thinking of the moment.

Over the course of my own career, I've certainly had moments when I decided to challenge the prevailing ideas. I did so in a variety of ways, including taking my concerns up the chain of command in writing or verbally; writing public articles for professional journals like the U.S. Naval Institute *Proceedings*; and—when I was finally in command myself in the latter days of my career—simply taking action to change something without seeking permission beforehand. An old Navy saying is that "it is better to seek forgiveness than to ask permission," and that is especially true if you are willing to put your professional reputation on the line. Sometimes I succeeded and sometimes I failed. Let me give an example of each.

One failure occurred during my time as commander of U.S. Southern Command. I felt strongly that the command structure was outmoded, too wedded to old ways of thinking about Latin America and the Caribbean. I was confident that we were not going to end up in a war down south; our missions had exclusively to do with counternarcotics, humanitarian relief, medical diplomacy, rule of law, training, and exercising collectively for counterterrorism operations. I therefore decided to change the command structure of the entire command, moving away from the traditional Napoleonic staff structure: J-1 = Personnel, J-2 = Intelligence, J-3 = Operations, and so on. This unorthodox move created huge consternation at many levels in the command. When I added the idea of appointing a deputy commander who was a former ambassador and a civilian, I feared people's heads were going to explode.

Undeterred by the reactions and certain of my personal views, I pressed ahead. And I failed. The staff of thousands seemed almost willfully confused by the changes; the other equivalent military organizations (the other combatant commanders) were discomfited because there was no longer a precise one-to-one relationship between all of our command staffs; and even my generally supportive boss in Washington (Secretary Bob Gates) didn't fully appreciate my maneuvers.

I left the command after it had operated a couple of years under the new structure, and my successor simply reverted to the old, traditional way of doing business. I respected his authority to do so, of course, but felt I had a wasted couple of years. But even though I failed to change the system, I was glad I had challenged it and thought independently, because in my next job, as Supreme Allied Commander of NATO, I was able to use the lessons I had learned.

The massive and bloated Cold War–level NATO staff of nearly 22,000 officers and senior enlisted personnel was unwieldy, cumbersome, and possessed too many layers of bureaucracy. So, I set out to reduce it by almost two-thirds, to around 8,000 personnel. This course of action had enormous political ramifications because the twenty-eight NATO member nations felt they had a stake in the positions they currently held. They liked the sense that "their" general was on the team in Brussels, Naples, the Netherlands, or Lisbon where the top headquarters were established. Most of them fought tooth and nail to avoid giving up any assignments.

But I had learned from the bruising I took at U.S. Southern Command. This time, I got buy-in at the very top, with the secretary general of NATO, and through him all the heads of state and government. It turned out that the ministers in London, Paris, Berlin, Rome, and all the capitals liked the idea of saving money by cutting personnel.

Second, I worked hard within the organization to explain what I was doing and why. I went personally to each of the headquarters of the various nations within the staff components. While not all were thrilled with cutting the size of their contingents, at least they were in the loop and understood the rationale for doing so. I worked hard with the media in each of the countries affected, and also with the U.S. Congress, which was quite happy with the reductions and willing to be helpful.

It was a far from perfect process, but ultimately it was a very successful one. We cut the standing headquarters' size in half and ended up with a lean, well-organized, and more deployable operation; and at the same time, we continued to conduct a huge combat operation in Afghanistan with more than 150,000 troops from more than 50 nations under our command. There were ongoing missions in the Balkans, on the sea for counterpiracy, and in cyber. And as we were concluding the reorganization in 2011, war broke out in Libya. That became the essential proving ground for the new concept.

Here's what I learned: thinking independently is hard and in many ways unnatural for humans. Sometimes I succeeded and other times it led me to failure. But if you want to see a guide to a situation where thinking for oneself is desperately necessary and requires real courage, look no further than Margaret Atwood's dark forest in *The Handmaid's Tale*. It has inspired me on many occasions since I first read it in 1985. That seems long ago, but much of what Atwood talks about continues to bubble through our society. As you read this difficult, twisted story, ask yourself, page after page, could I survive this? Only if you are brave enough to think independently.

CHAPTER ELEVEN

DREAM WITHOUT BOUNDARIES

Don Quixote

by *Miguel de Cervantes*

Perhaps to be too practical is madness.

When I was studying literature at the U.S. Naval Academy in the late twentieth century, one of my professors—a noted scholar of Hemingway and Dostoyevsky—said that all of Western literature can be traced to *Don Quixote*. There is a good deal of validity in that idea, but I would argue that *Don Quixote* is far more than a sort of yeast that gave birth to many later works of Western literature. For me, what matters most in this sprawling picaresque tale is the life philosophy it holds within its lengthy series of knightly adventures. The sequence of memorable moments populating this remarkable epic novel written in the early 1600s in Spain by Miguel de Cervantes reflect many of life's lessons.

The novel opens with a portrait of a knight whose position is at the lowest level of Spanish nobility in La Mancha, a dry but fertile region of central Spain. The hidalgo Alonso Quijano has spent years reading romantic tales of chivalry and romance—and as a direct result, has let slip his grip on reality. He decides his destiny is to become a knight-errant and to serve Spain, damsels in distress, the downtrodden, and other worthy causes. He takes the name Don Quixote de La Mancha and sets out to do those things; eventually he hires a peasant farmer, Sancho Panza, as his squire. The pairing is inspired. Don Quixote is quite mad, literally unhinged from reality; while Sancho Panza is the very epitome of real life: earthy, crude, clear-eyed, and cynical in the face of day-to-day challenges. During the course of the novel they form a powerful and mutually beneficial bond.

Don Quixote is roughly fifty years old, quite elderly for the 1600s. His fantasies convince him that he is an important and puissant knight, and he believes his broken-down old farm horse, Rosinante, is a knight's spirited charger. Don Quixote and Rosinante embark on a journey across Spain. In the opening portion of the novel, Don Quixote meets prostitutes whom he believes are courtly ladies and is mocked at various inns. He is beaten on several unfortunate occasions, but he is undeterred by these setbacks. At this point in the story Sancho Panza joins the quest, and the two set out again. The next adventure is the novel's most famous set-piece: Don Quixote's attack on several large windmills that he believes are evil giants who need to be subdued.

Over the course of the next months, Don Quixote and Sancho are beset by challenges. They are fleeced in various inns, engage in an epic battle with wineskins, and are imprisoned for freeing galley slaves. Don Quixote is often beaten, usually cheated, and thoroughly mocked. And yet as part one ends, he returns home undaunted by the distinctly disappointing aspects of his adventures. In the second part of the novel (which Cervantes wrote a decade later, probably by popular demand), Sancho and Don Quixote eventually encounter Dulcinea, the mythical damsel Don Quixote originally set out to save. Various characters, some of whom are clearly aware of Don Quixote's adventures in part one of the novel, decide to play along with his fantasies. Eventually our knight-errant is defeated in battle near Barcelona and is forced by the code of chivalry to cease his quest for at least a year.

> "Destiny guides our fortunes more favorably than we could have expected."

As they slowly make their way back to La Mancha, Don Quixote and Sancho Panza are bowed but not defeated. Don Quixote says he will retire and become a shepherd, but instead he ends up quietly taking to his bed in the home in which we first met him. After suffering an illness, he awakens as if from a long dream and has shed his identity as Don Quixote. He embraces his true and original identity as Alonso Quijano and foreswears the kind of adventures that had been at the heart of his quest, going so far as to write into his will that his niece will lose her heritance should she marry a man who is an obsessive reader of books of chivalry.

There is an almost endless amount of wisdom and advice in *Don Quixote*. I have read it three separate times in my life, as well as seeing the 1972 film *Man of La Mancha*, and I took away different lessons each time.

My first encounter with the novel was when I was a midshipman at the Naval Academy, where the comedy and dark humor of the tale appealed deeply to me. I took a battered copy of the book to sea with me and occasionally dipped into it to escape from the day-to-day grind of sea duty. Of particular note to me then, of course, was the prolonged scene of Don Quixote attacking the oblivious windmills. On plenty of occasions as a junior officer, I likewise found myself tilting at the windmills of the stodgy and conservative surface Navy. Cervantes' words helped focus my own quest to continue, despite the frequent defeats and setbacks. The book truly encouraged a young and idealistic junior officer to dream without boundaries. As Cervantes says in the novel, "To surrender dreams—this may be madness."

The second time I read the book I was a destroyer captain in my late thirties, and it took on a very different tone and meaning to me. I began to read it as a novel of Don Quixote's journey, with its many stopping points and side adventures—like Homer's *Odyssey*, the story of a traveler who would never fully comprehend what was around the next turn on a long, winding road. It helped me understand that there is seldom a final, certain resolution to the series of challenges life puts in our path.

As a ship's commanding officer in the early 1990s, I was leading hundreds of Sailors into operations off the coast of Haiti, in the waters off the Balkans at the height of that conflict, and all the way to the very northern waters of the Arabian Gulf in response to Saddam Hussein's invasion of Kuwait. We never knew where or when the next crisis would spring up, nor exactly what we would need to do to confront it. Like Don Quixote, we had our share of small victories and painful defeats—capturing an arms smuggler one fine morning in the Adriatic Sea and nearly running aground in the Suez Canal a few days later, for example. *Don Quixote* helped me to appreciate the beauty of the journey despite the failures and defeats that came along the way. I learned to recognize that our dreams may or may not come true; but if we are to live life to the fullest extent, we should not cut short our capacity to continue the journey and must, above all, remain open to our imagination—much as that Spanish knight did four centuries ago.

At that stage of my life the novel reminded me that the voyage itself was everything. The Greek poet C. P. Cavafy echoed that philosophy centuries later in his classic work *Ithaka*. Named for the island toward which Odysseus spent a decade sailing after the end of the Trojan War, the poem's cadences and lyrics remind us of the unpredictability and power of the voyage—and that the destination in many cases is less important than the voyage itself:

> Hope that your road is a long one.
> May there be many summer mornings when,
> with what pleasure, what joy,
> you enter harbors you're seeing for the first time.
>
> Keep Ithaka always in your mind.
> Arriving there is what you're destined for.
> But don't hurry the journey at all.
> Better if it lasts for years.

Cervantes says it best in the voice of the pragmatist Sancho Panza, who advises with tongue slightly in cheek: "Take my advice and live for a long, long time. Because the maddest thing a man can do in this life is to let himself die."

Finally, this remarkable piece of literature came alive again in a third reading as I dusted off the admiral's bookshelf—but in a very different way. Today when I read about Don Quixote at the end of the novel, returned to his roots, reverting to his original self, and embracing the reality of his life, I am reminded that life has a way of slowing us down and allowing us to sum up all that has happened to us.

If we are lucky, as we near the end of our life's journey we can look back and be at peace with all we have done. Each of us will remember times of real elation and excitement as some remarkable dream came true, from the joy of a marriage to gaining a coveted promotion. We are equally likely to remember moments of immense sorrow and failure, perhaps the death of a beloved relative or being disciplined for a significant mistake. In the same year, I pinned on the star of a rear admiral and was soon thereafter nearly killed in the September 11 attack on the Pentagon. In many ways, at the heart of *Don Quixote* is the human capacity to undergo and survive immense heartache, physical pain, and emotional suffering—much of it caused by our own human tendency for self-deception. It is a novel that helps us remember Rudyard Kipling's definition of maturity in the poem "If":

> If you can meet with Triumph and Disaster
> And treat those two imposters just the same.

In many ways, the line between our tragedies and our successes is very thin indeed. Looking back on my voyage thus far, I can see both very clearly. A sense of perspective and knowing that life is going to have a share of both helps me balance my judgments about not only my own life but those of the people around me. As Cervantes says, "It's up to brave hearts . . . to be patient when things are going badly, as well as being happy when they're going when they're going well."

In the end, the reason I put *Don Quixote* in *The Admiral's Bookshelf* is a combination of all three readings: it is a novel that can impart a sense of the dark comedy we all deal with in our daily lives; underscore for us that the voyage will be a long, winding, and unpredictable affair; and help us understand that the further we sail in our lives, the more value there is in keeping a sense of perspective on the breathless moments of triumph and disaster that inevitably appear in the long throw of our life's voyage. No other single book can offer so much to a thoughtful reader. Brave hearts indeed.

CHAPTER TWELVE

BE PATIENT

The Odyssey
by Homer

---

*Ah how shameless—the way these
mortals blame the gods.*

I first encountered Ulysses and his long voyage home when I was a young boy in Athens, Greece. My father, a career officer in the U.S. Marine Corps, was Greek American and fluent in the language. He didn't speak English until he started public school, having been raised in a Greek community in eastern Pennsylvania. Thus, the Corps sent him to be a naval attaché to the American embassy in Athens in the early 1960s. As part of our preparations to move to Greece, he ensured that I received an appropriate grounding in Greek mythology, history, and that curious blend of the two represented by Homer's epic poems about the Trojan War and its aftermath.

While I did not appreciate their importance to Western literature at the time, I was later to learn much more about Homer's stories. Composed of two separate epics, *The Iliad* and *The Odyssey*, the poems were probably written around 2,800 years ago and might (or might not) have been composed separately. Almost certainly they were part of an oral tradition of storytelling passed along from bard to bard over the long centuries. Each of the volumes comprises twenty-four books, and each volume covers roughly a decade. *The Iliad* describes the end of the ten-year Trojan War, in which the Greek city-states came together to attack their rival city-state, Troy, after Helen, the wife of one Greek king, Menelaus, was stolen by the Trojan prince Paris. *The Odyssey* then follows the voyage of Odysseus, the king of the small island kingdom of Ithaca, as he battles his way home over yet another ten-year period.

To an eleven-year-old boy surrounded by the ruins of ancient Greece, reading Homer in an abridged but very richly illustrated edition was bliss. I could look from the balcony of our home in the suburbs of Athens and see the Parthenon in the fading sunset light as I turned the pages. I began with *The Iliad*, the earlier of the two epics, which deals with the Trojan War itself. That story tells of the ending of the long war between Greeks and Trojans that concludes with the Greeks' conquest of Troy, the destruction of that city, the death of the Greek warrior-hero Achilles, and the departure of the Greeks from what is today western Turkey to return to their various homes across Greece. The battle scenes of *The Iliad* stirred me, and the tragic outcomes—for the Trojans but also for many of the Greeks—moved me as well. It is a book of war, swords, armor, mysterious gods who interfere for various reasons, treachery, love, and tragedy. I found it deeply entertaining and exciting.

When I put down *The Iliad* and picked up *The Odyssey*, I was ready for a new adventure and hoping for more great battles, soldiers, kings, and princes. Instead, I discovered a very different kind of book. *The Odyssey* describes a long, long voyage by a very homesick man, Odysseus, desperate to return to his hearth and home. He longs to be reunited with his wise, beautiful, and beloved wife, Penelope, and to see his young son, Telemachus. But he angered the gods in the final days of the war, and the Trojan-favoring residents of Mount Olympus have a considerable axe to grind with our protagonist and throw many obstacles in his path. He finally achieves his heart's desire and reaches Ithaca, only to find that a final challenge awaits before he can return to his old life.

As *The Odyssey* opens, Odysseus is facing the anger of Poseidon, the god of the oceans, while back home in Ithaca, Penelope and Telemachus have their own problems. Believing Odysseus dead, a hundred suitors are besieging the queen, demanding her hand, eating all the palace's food and wine, and plotting against Telemachus, the presumptive heir to the throne.

After escaping from the demigoddess Calypso after years in captivity, Odysseus has been shipwrecked on another island of the Phaeacians. He meets the island's king and queen and recounts the story of his initial departure from Troy with twelve ships and his adventures up to being imprisoned by Calypso.

The initial part of the voyage includes time among the lotus-eaters, who can make sailors forget their dreams of home. Next, Odysseus and his men land on another island where they anger a son of the powerful god Poseidon, who curses them. This leads to a series of misadventures, including losing the bag of sacred winds given to Odysseus by the god of wind, Aeolus; an encounter with cannibals; and a landing on the island of the demigoddess and witch Circe. She changes many of his men into pigs, but Odysseus ultimately outwits her, rescues his men, and seduces Circe. They stay a year with her until she regretfully sends them on their way with directions and hope.

> "Where have you been wandering, and in what countries have you travelled? Tell us of the peoples themselves, and of their cities—who were hostile, savage and uncivilized, and who were hospitable and humane."

But the obstacles continue to appear. Sailing to the edge of the world, Odysseus communes with the shade of his mother, sacrifices to the dead, and is advised regarding events in Ithaca. This spurs his already burning desire to return to his kingdom, and he sets sail once again. The ships sail by the land of the sirens, whose song seduces men into madness—but Odysseus has his men plug their ears with beeswax. They safely navigate the treacherous waters between a deadly whirlpool, Charybdis, and a monster with six heads, Scylla. Eventually Odysseus and his men land on the island of Thrinacia, where the men—unbeknownst to him—eat the sacred cattle of the god Helios. A furious Zeus destroys all of the ships and kills the men, and Odysseus washes ashore on Ogygia and becomes the lover/prisoner of Calypso.

The final portion of *The Odyssey* deals with Odysseus' return to Ithaca. There he is aided by the goddess Minerva, reunites with Telemachus, slays his wife's suitors in a final, gory set-piece, hangs the twelve slave girls who betrayed Penelope, and convinces Penelope that he is indeed the husband who sailed off to war twenty years earlier. The long voyage is done, and the hero-king is resettled on the throne and happily in the arms of his beautiful queen with his adoring son and heir at his side.

I have reread *The Odyssey* as an adult several times and continue to be struck by the creativity of the individual adventures embedded in the overall story. Three things stand out about this extraordinary tale.

The first is the deep nautical roots of the story. At heart, it is a sea voyage through the first waters conquered by civilized humans, the Mediterranean. As a naval officer, every time I sailed through the Strait of Gibraltar (known in antiquity as the Pillars of Hercules), I would marvel at the geography of the tale. While the parallels are inexact, there is reason to believe that the land of the lotus-eaters was present-day Corfu, an island off the western coast of Greece. The narrow passage between Scylla and Charybdis might have been the difficult seaway between Sicily and mainland Italy. Gibraltar could have been the western edge of the world, near the gates to Hades, where Odysseus saw his mother again. The Phaeacians could have been Phoenicians, and of course Ithaka is an actual island today.

I remember sailing through the Strait of Messina as a young destroyer captain on a cold October day with a mistral blowing. The strait is between the western tip of the Calabrian Peninsula and the eastern tip of Sicily, the largest island in the Mediterranean. The strait therefore connects the Ionian Sea with the central Mediterranean. At its narrowest point, it is not even two miles wide—very close quarters for an eight-thousand-ton destroyer. In addition to being a challenging little stretch of water given the proximity of unforgiving land on both sides, there are extremely powerful rip tides and a weird natural whirlpool that is probably the source of the myths of Scylla (Sicily's name derives from that feature) and Charybdis. When I sailed through for the first time, the dangers Odysseus encountered in *The Odyssey* were very much on my mind, but the most frightening sights were the Italian ferry boat captains. They drive those ferries at extremely high speeds and complacently cut in front of larger ships. As the third one cut directly in front of me on that winter's day, I thought to myself I'd rather be facing a six-headed monster than any more of these brazen boat captains. *The Odyssey* is full of shipwrecks, collisions, harsh storms, bad anchorages, and sea battles, and for that reason alone it deserves a spot on *The Admiral's Bookshelf.*

But the second, and far more important, central lesson of *The Odyssey* is the importance of appreciating our life's voyage and the need to be patient in achieving our goals. Much like Cervantes' *Don Quixote,* which was clearly influenced by the journey of Odysseus, Homer's epic is about the tension between our desire to find our homeport and the joy of adventure. We must be both resilient and patient if we are to overcome the challenges that life will present. In that sense, *The Odyssey* is a fine sea chart to use in the voyage of life. In the course of my long naval career, I often reflected on the careers of contemporaries and Naval Academy classmates who decided to get out of the Navy and go to graduate school, typically to get a law or MBA degree, or directly into business. It was hard not to envy the high speed with which their careers accelerated, doubling and tripling my meager Navy pay in just a few years and quickly climbing the ladders of their professions. My advance through the Navy was a long, slow voyage with the necessity of proving myself both at sea and ashore all along the way. A naval officer could never skip the steps of being a division officer, a department head, an executive officer, a commanding officer, or a commodore en route to making rear admiral. At sea, as the saying goes, it takes ten years to get ten years of experience. Likewise, I found the need to move deliberately and slowly up the ladder ashore in various jobs.

A career in the military requires patience. It is exciting, adventurous, and fulfilling, and I wouldn't trade a minute of it. But succeeding means realizing that the voyage will take time. It is a long, slow journey to even become a ship captain, and it should be. But when I would get impatient, which I often did in the second and third years as a department head, for example, I could look to the voyage of Odysseus. I am certainly no Greek hero, but I learned in reading about one how important patience can and must be for any truly worthwhile pursuit.

Third, and finally, *The Odyssey* is about how we will judge our lives at the end of our individual voyages. It is this theme that is less appreciated, and one that I fully realized only as I sailed into my sixth decade of life. And this lesson has to do, interestingly, with what happens to Odysseus *after* he returns to his beloved kingdom of Ithaca. And this moves us beyond the tale told by Homer and into two other important works.

> **"There is a time for making speeches, and a time for going to bed."**

The first is another extraordinary and seminal work, *The Inferno* by Dante Alighieri. In the twenty-sixth canto of *The Inferno*, the narrator, Dante, encounters Odysseus in the eighth circle of hell. Here he learns that Odysseus never returned to Ithaca at all but instead continued to wander for all of his days on earth. This new ending is a testament to the wanderlust at the center of Homer's story. In my own life, this occurred to me after I finally retired from the Navy after thirty-seven years of service. I hung up my dress blues and thought about just stopping there. Many of my contemporaries decided to play golf, sit on a few corporate boards, maybe do some volunteer work. Had I not achieved all that I wanted in becoming a four-star admiral and Supreme Allied Commander? Had I not figuratively returned to my Ithaca after achieving what I set out to do?

What I realized as I thought about my place in the world was simple: there was much more left to do. All of my failures and shortcomings along the Navy voyage were merely signposts and suggestions for what would come next. I turned to a life mentor, former secretary of defense Bob Gates, and asked his advice. "Well, Jim," he said, "you've always loved mentoring sailors. Have you thought about becoming an educator?" So, I set out to try a new role in that world.

I made many, many mistakes in transitioning from the military to higher education, from misunderstanding the needs of graduate students to failing to recognize and respect the power (and occasional fury) of the tenured faculty. On my five-year journey through the world of the American university I met my share of mythical monsters and unforgiving gods. Reading *The Odyssey* and Dante's poignant depiction of Odysseus in *The Inferno* helped me have the patience for that new world and the spirit of hope to sail into it.

The poem "Ulysses" by Alfred Lord Tennyson, the poet laureate of Victorian England, gives us yet another ending to Odysseus' story. Written in the mid-nineteenth century, the poem conjures up a Ulysses who does in fact return to Ithaca, conquer the vile suitors, reunite with Penelope, and then invest his kingdom in Telemachus. But the twist is that after having spent twenty years in war and adventuring on the sea, he "cannot rest from travel." Old as he is, he decides to return to the adventurous life and sail again, leaving the kingdom in the hands of Telemachus.

"Ulysses" is a beautiful, heartbreaking, hopeful, and deeply meaningful poem about how Odysseus made the choice to forsake a quiet retirement. His boredom in this retirement is palpable (he is "an idle king"), and his nostalgia for the life of adventure and the excitement of the journey glitters in his mind ("I cannot rest from travel: I will drink life to the lees"). Tempted by his memories, Odysseus simply cannot resist the urge to go back into the arena of life:

> All experience is an arch wherethro'
> Gleams that untravell'd world whose margin fades
> For ever and forever when I move.

He acknowledges that he is much diminished and weakened by time, and yet his life is far from over:

> Old age hath yet his honour and his toil;
> Death closes all: but something ere the end,
> Some work of noble note, may yet be done.

As the poem closes, we stand alongside the man with whom we sailed throughout Homer's long epic poem. This wily, pragmatic Greek warrior and sailor—the cleverest of all the Greeks, inventor of the Trojan Horse; a sailor of the uncharted world; a favorite and an enemy of the gods—knows in his heart two things: that he is older and weaker than he was, and there still remains something for him to accomplish. Thus, this poem, which is a perfect coda to *The Odyssey* itself, concludes with the lines:

> We are not now that strength which in old days
> Moved earth and heaven, that which we are, we are;
> One equal temper of heroic hearts,
> Made weak by time and fate, but strong in will
> To strive, to seek, to find, and not to yield

As I look back over the voyage of my life, both at sea and ashore, I am still moved by the story of Odysseus. He was unafraid to grasp life with both hands, to battle and fight his way to achieve the goals he set for himself. When I add to the epic by Homer the pitch-perfect depiction of Odysseus' later life by

Tennyson, I feel the need as well to continue to engage with the world. Since leaving higher education I've taken an entirely new role in global affairs at an international financial firm. It is a third leg of my voyage, a set of new experiences where I both succeed and fail. Part of what inspired me to take on yet another full-time role was reading Tennyson's poem, with its deep echoes of both the sea and the story of Odysseus.

I seldom pull out *The Odyssey* these days; it is in many ways a young person's poem. But I often reread Tennyson's poem, which captures a spirit and a hope for adventures still to come that appeal to this senior sailor. I reproduce it below along with my advice to be patient in all the voyages of your life and unafraid to set a new course, wherever you are in the journey.

"Ulysses" by Alfred, Lord Tennyson

It little profits that an idle king,
By this still hearth, among these barren crags,
Match'd with an aged wife, I mete and dole
Unequal laws unto a savage race,
That hoard, and sleep, and feed, and know not me.
I cannot rest from travel: I will drink
Life to the lees: All times I have enjoy'd
Greatly, have suffer'd greatly, both with those
That loved me, and alone, on shore, and when
Thro' scudding drifts the rainy Hyades
Vext the dim sea: I am become a name;
For always roaming with a hungry heart
Much have I seen and known; cities of men
And manners, climates, councils, governments,
Myself not least, but honour'd of them all;
And drunk delight of battle with my peers,

Far on the ringing plains of windy Troy.
I am a part of all that I have met;
Yet all experience is an arch wherethro'
Gleams that untravell'd world whose margin fades
For ever and forever when I move.
How dull it is to pause, to make an end,
To rust unburnish'd, not to shine in use!
As tho' to breathe were life! Life piled on life
Were all too little, and of one to me
Little remains: but every hour is saved
From that eternal silence, something more,
A bringer of new things; and vile it were
For some three suns to store and hoard myself,
And this gray spirit yearning in desire
To follow knowledge like a sinking star,
Beyond the utmost bound of human thought.

This is my son, mine own Telemachus,
To whom I leave the sceptre and the isle—
Well-loved of me, discerning to fulfil
This labour, by slow prudence to make mild
A rugged people, and thro' soft degrees
Subdue them to the useful and the good.
Most blameless is he, centred in the sphere
Of common duties, decent not to fail
In offices of tenderness, and pay
Meet adoration to my household gods,
When I am gone. He works his work, I mine.

There lies the port; the vessel puffs her sail:
There gloom the dark, broad seas. My mariners,
Souls that have toil'd, and wrought, and thought with me—

That ever with a frolic welcome took
The thunder and the sunshine, and opposed
Free hearts, free foreheads—you and I are old;
Old age hath yet his honour and his toil;
Death closes all: but something ere the end,
Some work of noble note, may yet be done,
Not unbecoming men that strove with Gods.
The lights begin to twinkle from the rocks:
The long day wanes: the slow moon climbs: the deep
Moans round with many voices. Come, my friends,
'Tis is not too late to seek a newer world.
Push off, and sitting well in order smite
The sounding furrows; for my purpose holds
To sail beyond the sunset, and the baths
Of all the western stars, until I die.
It may be that the gulfs will wash us down:
It may be we shall touch the Happy Isles,
And see the great Achilles, whom we knew.
Tho' much is taken, much abides; and tho'
We are not now that strength which in old days
Moved earth and heaven, that which we are, we are;
One equal temper of heroic hearts,
Made weak by time and fate, but strong in will
To strive, to seek, to find, and not to yield.

CHAPTER THIRTEEN

BALANCE THE TACTICAL WITH THE STRATEGIC

The Art of War

by Sun Tzu

> All men can see these tactics whereby I conquer, but what none can see is the strategy out of which victory is evolved.

Sun Tzu's immortal classic, *The Art of War*, first fell into my possession in the summer of 1972 as part of the stack of textbooks issued to every incoming freshman at the U.S. Naval Academy. Ironically, it was alongside another paperback, *The Elements of Style*, that would also have an enormous influence on my career. As I learned more about both books, it was clear to me that each had a role in creating winning strategies—via the pen in the case of *Elements of Style*, and the sword in the case of

Sun Tzu. That paperback, battered by use and its cover stained by coffee cups, has been with me for nearly fifty years.

Written sometime around the fifth century BC, *The Art of War* is exactly what the title says: a comprehensive treatise on the conduct of combat both on a small tactical scale and at the broad strategic level. The authorship is a bit obscure given the distance of time but is generally attributed to Sun Tzu (which can be translated as "master of the sun" or "sun master"). It has passed through many translations and adaptations but has always retained its place as the most influential of the Asian texts on war. At its most prosaic level, the book describes Chinese weapons, military formations, tactics, and discipline. It also played an early role in laying out the necessity of spying on the enemy and synthesizing the information—what we today think of as information warfare—critical to a successful military campaign.

There are only thirteen chapters in this short book, which is written in a style that lends itself to the extraction of pithy quotes that can then be debated for their ultimate meaning. Here's a quick summary of the chapters and essential meanings, using my own chosen titles given the variety of translations.

> *Chapter 1—Planning.* Look first at the basic facts of the military challenge: terrain, leadership, time of the year. War is the deadliest of human endeavors, and the most dangerous.
>
> *Chapter 2—Fighting.* "Economy" is an important consideration in warfare; winning quickly and balancing resources are both paramount. Sun Tzu also emphasizes the distinction between tactical successes and failures against the larger strategic objectives of war. This balance between tactical and strategic is at the heart of *The Art of War.*

Chapter 3—Attack. Warfare is a team activity. Strength comes from unity, especially in active warfare. Five key factors are offense, strategy, alliances, military forces, and cities.

Chapter 4—Tactics. Sun Tzu shifts to defense, exploring how best to dispose forces, keep safe bastions, and create opportunities for offense while denying them to the enemy.

Chapter 5—Energy. Timing and innovation are keys to creating momentum for an attacking force; that is, its combat energy.

Chapter 6—Weakness and Strength. The key to victory often is finding the balance between your enemy's weak points and your own strength. This chapter is reminiscent of ancient individual martial arts such as jujitsu and karate that stress using an enemy's strength against him.

Chapter 7—Maneuver. This chapter is quite similar to the discussions the German master strategist, Clausewitz, pursued about the vital importance of maneuvering an army intelligently and forcefully. By the way, all of these points are focused on land warfare, but they apply equally in sea, air, space, and cyber.

Chapter 8—Variation and Surprise. Explores, through "nine variations," the need to be flexible and unpredictable in deploying military force.

Chapter 9—Logistics and Movement. Being able to maneuver forces requires capable field operations, to include keeping supplies moving quickly and efficiently to support units in the field.

Chapter 10—Terrain. The chapter defines "six types of terrain" and how a master general responds to changing land conditions. Three areas of resistance are distance, dangers, and barriers.

Chapter 11—Nine Situations. This chapter provides a handy overview of stages in a campaign and some classic reactions. A campaign is a bit like a chess stratagem, to which this chapter is often compared.

Chapter 12—Firepower in War. This chapter, which depicts types of targets and responses to them, is not as useful as the other chapters, as it tends to be tied specifically to ancient systems; nonetheless, it is worth reading in order to apply its lessons to the modern world.

Chapter 13—Spies. This final chapter reads like a page out of a CIA manual for supporting forces in combat. Accurate information is crucial in the conduct of war. Sun Tzu describes the five types of intelligence and how to best capture them.

In my nearly forty-year career in the military, I carried the lessons of that little paperback book forward in both peace and war. Despite the "war" in the title, I've found that the key principles pertain whether you are locked into active combat in the high mountains of Afghanistan; in interagency bureaucratic warfare in Washington between Defense, State, and the NSC; or running a graduate school of law and diplomacy and negotiating with a difficult faculty. Let me give you a few examples.

Perhaps the most frequently repeated aphorism from Sun Tzu's work, and deservedly so, is: "The greatest victory is that which requires no battle." He means we should put aside the passion and anger attendant to our conflicts and instead seek to find diplomatic win-win outcomes. In my personal experience, the best example of this was in the long guerrilla war in Colombia. As Commander, U.S. Southern Command, I watched various Colombian governments struggle with the dangerous insurgency mounted by the FARC guerrillas. There was never going to be a decisive battle; the Colombians had to defeat them through negotiations.

This was ultimately accomplished by Juan Manal Santos, who was my good friend and wartime colleague when he was minister of defense and I was the U.S. four-star focused on the war. We had many conversations about finding a path to a diplomatic outcome—moving beyond the five decades of tactical gridlock to a strategic outcome. Eventually Minister Santos became President Santos and negotiated a peace agreement. It is not perfect, and aspects of it continue to be challenging, but he was deservedly awarded the Nobel Peace Prize. As I watched him accept the award, I thought, *here is Sun Tzu come to life*.

A second famous quote that will reverberate in my head for the rest of my life—because I failed to heed it—is this: "If you know the enemy and know yourself, you need not fear the result of a hundred battles. If you know yourself, but not the enemy, for every victory gained you will also suffer a defeat. If you know neither the enemy nor yourself, you will succumb in every battle."

The wisdom of this quote rings true and clear when I think back to my role as Supreme Allied Commander of NATO and the execution of our failed mission in Afghanistan. We never truly understood the Taliban—the measure of their determination, resourcefulness, and wiliness. They told us themselves, "You Americans have all the watches, but we have all the time."

For a long time, I think we did know ourselves, and we managed to fight a series of draws on the battlefields of that tragic nation. We were able to expel the Taliban from much of the country and bring more than 80 percent of the population under government and allied control. We achieved successes in everything from medical outreach to life expectancy to schooling for women and girls. But ultimately, we in the West failed to know ourselves; nor did we ever really know the Taliban; and thus—as

Sun Tzu would have predicted—we ended ignominiously. Deep knowledge about both yourself and your opponents is crucial to success in any human endeavor.

Another quote from Sun Tzu that I've carried from the military to other parts of my career is quite short: "All warfare is based on deception." Quite simply, it means that in any competition, you have to protect the base of your own intelligence (maintaining the high ground in information warfare) while at the same time penetrating the enemy's knowledge base. We did this very successfully while I was NATO commander in defeating the (admittedly hapless) forces of Libyan dictator Muammar Khadafy. We were able not only to protect our vital intelligence but also to repeatedly convince Khadafy that we were shifting combat power away from our real objectives. This caused him to change the location of his air defense and other systems and opened his forces up to punishing strikes. It was a David and Goliath battle, but in this case, as the Goliath figure, we had both the size and the intelligence to win—based on being able to deceive our opponent.

An often-overlooked quote from Sun Tzu can close this small sample of the wisdom of this volume: "When on death ground, fight." We think of Sun Tzu as the master of deception, winner of diplomatic victories, a battle master who never actually needed to draw his sword to conquer an opponent. But at one point in *The Art of War* he points out that sometimes all the clever stratagems may fail, and in that dire moment, which he calls the "death ground," you must fight—and fight hard. The death ground is the worst place to find yourself in battle.

The closest I've come to that, I suppose, was in the Pentagon on 9/11. As I stood a few hundred feet from the shattered side of the Pentagon, knowing that hundreds of my shipmates on the Department of Defense staff were dead or wounded inside,

I knew I was on my personal death ground. As a one-star rear admiral I wasn't high enough in the hierarchy to really matter, but I made the same two vows my shipmates throughout the armed forces made.

First, we would find and kill those who had attacked us. There was no doubt of that in my mind. We were not going to negotiate a win-win outcome. We'd find them and kill them. Second, and more important, I would give my life, as would every member of the U.S. armed forces, to prevent another attack like 9/11, which killed thousands of innocent civilians. We took Sun Tzu's maxim to heart: when on death ground, fight. And for the next twenty years we did exactly that. We found and killed Osama bin Laden and thousands of his followers. And we succeeded in preventing another attack on the homeland throughout those decades, working with our partners in the intelligence and law enforcement communities and the Department of Homeland Security, itself a creation of the 9/11 attacks.

Central to *The Art of War* is the need to balance the tactical and the strategic aspects of the conflict; in other words, to balance the minute details of a given situation with the big-picture outcome you are seeking. A leader cannot ignore either. Here I think of that superb politician Franklin Delano Roosevelt. He knew the minutiae of domestic politics, including the names of the Democratic Party chairmen in most of the counties in the United States, and at the same time he managed to wrangle notoriously difficult personalities like De Gaulle, Churchill, and Stalin into a grand strategic alliance at the height of World War II. I doubt he ever read Sun Tzu, but as a war leader he found that crucial balance between tactics and strategy.

Even today, as I continue my career in international business, I often refer to that old, red-covered copy of *The Art of War*. The stakes are not as high now, thankfully, and there is no literal "death ground." But the fundamental principles of this slim, powerful volume still pertain: seek win-win outcomes; fight hard when the stakes are the highest and there is no obvious outcome; be cleverer than your opponent; cherish good intelligence; know yourself and study your opponent. Those fine principles have stood me in good stead in the fields of fire as a military officer, ashore as a leader in higher education, and today in international business and finance. As usual, I make my share of mistakes, but when I find myself in a situation where things aren't going my way, I pull out *The Art of War* and work to try to apply its wisdom. It has saved me many a time.

CHAPTER FOURTEEN

MENTOR WILLINGLY

To Kill a Mockingbird

by Harper Lee

> You never really understand a person until you consider things from his point of view . . . until you climb into his skin and walk around in it.
>
> —Atticus Finch

This is the book on *The Admiral's Bookshelf* that most people will have already read. It is a staple in virtually every middle school or early high school English class, and deservedly so. So, many young people in their early teens encounter this remarkable book, and most of them enjoy it greatly. It jogs some of their thinking about race, justice, and growing up. Then they get back on TikTok, or at best turn to *The Great Gatsby*. I'm tempted to say it is a book that is wasted on the young, but even a passing exposure in your teens is beneficial and meaningful. But while it is not entirely wasted on the young, this masterpiece of American literature is really a book to be reread and savored much later in life.

I've reread *To Kill a Mockingbird* four times, roughly once a decade starting in my thirties. It never fails to move me deeply. And each time I read it, I also watched the fine 1962 black-and-white film starring Gregory Peck as Atticus Finch, a role for which he deservedly received the Academy Award for Best Actor. Indeed, the film was nominated for eight Oscars, and won three. It is one of the few truly powerful screen adaptions of an extraordinary novel. While the movie misses some of the nuances and characters important to the novel, it is an excellent companion piece to Harper Lee's book.

The novel was published in 1960 and immediately garnered both commercial and critical success. It won the Pulitzer Prize for fiction in 1961 and has been a staple of American literature since its release. Harper Lee incorporated into it much of what she experienced growing up in the American South in the 1930s, including some of the courtroom scenes that lie at the heart of the book.

The book is narrated by Jean Louise Finch, known as "Scout," who is only six as the story opens. She and her older brother Jem live with their father, a widowed lawyer named Atticus Finch. The family's cook and maid, Calpurnia, has helped Atticus raise the children since the death of their mother. Another key character is the mysterious Boo Radley (played by a young Robert Duvall in the film), a reclusive neighbor who develops an odd but affectionate relationship with the children. They have never seen Boo, but he occasionally leaves them gifts in a small tree outside his home.

The courtroom drama at the heart of the novel centers on a Black man, Tom Robinson, who is accused of raping a white woman, Mayella Ewell. The white citizens of the town assume that Tom is guilty, given his race, and are angry and disappointed when Atticus decides to defend Tom at his trial. When a group of white men attempt to lynch Tom, Atticus faces them down in front of the jail. But it is Scout, innocently talking to one of the adult men present, who defuses the dangerous moment.

As the trial unfolds, it becomes clear that Mayella and her father, Bob Ewell, are lying, and that it was Mayella who initiated contact with Tom. Despite Atticus' heroic defense, the jury of all white men votes to convict Tom. Although Atticus has hopes of overturning the verdict on appeal, Tom is shot and killed while supposedly trying to escape captivity before Atticus can act.

Following Tom's death, Bob Ewell vows to wreak revenge on Atticus and his family for destroying his reputation and Mayella's at the trial. He attacks Scout and Jem while they are out trick-or-treating, hurting both of them and breaking Jem's arm, but a mysterious man comes to the children's rescue. That man, we soon learn, is Boo, the Finches' mysterious next-door neighbor.

Each time I reread the novel I find myself concentrating on a different element of the story. The book contains four powerful and interwoven themes. The first and most obvious focus of the book illuminates the blatant racism of America in the 1930s (and during Harper Lee's time as well). From the segregated balcony where Blacks are required to confine themselves during the trial to the harsh language and preconceived notions of the white population, it is clear that racism is at the heart of Harper Lee's criticisms. Atticus tells his children, "As you grow older, you'll see white men cheat black men every day of your life but let me tell you something and don't you forget it—whenever a white man does that to a black man, no matter who he is, how rich he is, or how fine a family he comes from, that white man is trash."

A second theme, interwoven with the pernicious elements of racism, is the flawed American judicial system. As a lawyer himself, Atticus sees these flaws with near complete clarity. He knows that Tom is not going to get a fair trial. But at the same time, he continues to hold hope for the system as an institution that offers at least some measure of justice.

He says to the jury, "But there is one way in this country in which all men are created equal—there is one human institution that makes a pauper the equal of a Rockefeller, the stupid man the equal of an Einstein, and the ignorant man the equal of any college president. That institution, gentlemen, is a court. It can be the Supreme Court of the United States or the humblest JP court in the land, or this honorable court which you serve."

Atticus goes on to conclude: "Our courts have their faults as does any human institution, but in this country our courts are the great levelers, and in our courts all men are created equal." Like Atticus, I wish that were uniformly true. But as strongly as he articulates these hopes, by the end of the novel Atticus is forced to see the complete failure of the judicial system: an unfair conviction and finally the nonjudicial killing of an innocent Black man.

The third—and perhaps the most personal theme of the work for me—is the importance of mentoring. Atticus, above all else, is a loving father and mentor who wants his children to be fair, honest, unbiased, and intelligent observers of what can be a flawed and dangerous world. "There's a lot of ugly things in this world," he tells Scout and Jem. "I wish I could keep 'em all away from you. That's never possible." Throughout the novel, he talks to Scout about the world, her important place in it, and the kind of a young woman he wants her to be.

One of his constant themes as a mentor is the need for his children to understand others by figuratively walking in their shoes. "You never really understand a person until you consider things from his point of view," he tells them, ". . . until you climb into his skin and walk around in it." Atticus constantly seeks to understand how both his friends and his opponents are thinking. This is a powerful lesson to impart as a mentor.

Another key element of his mentorship is teaching his children to do the hard right thing, regardless of how it might be perceived by others, rather than the easy wrong one, even when defeat is certain. "Simply because we were licked a hundred years before we started is no reason for us not to try to win," he insists.

> **"The one thing that doesn't abide by majority rule is a person's conscience."**

He takes on the highly unpopular defense of an accused Black man because he knows it is the right thing to do, even as he recognizes the real danger to his family and his finances. But as he says, "Before I can live with other folks, I've got to live with myself."

I've tried to be a good mentor along my own voyage, and some of the most important precepts I followed came straight from *To Kill a Mockingbird*. When I've been most effective, it is because I've tried to be unemotional and honest with my mentees. For example, in my first command at sea, a guided missile destroyer, I had an officer I just didn't like: he was arrogant, harsh with his subordinates, and tried to run his department through creating an atmosphere of crisis. I've always felt that approach—anger, unreasonable demands, demeaning subordinates—is doomed to failure.

I tried hard to work with him to improve his leadership skills, and along the way nearly lost my own temper with him several times. I even asked him to read *To Kill a Mockingbird* and tried coaching him using Atticus Finch as a role model. Nothing worked. He had immense talent and was an excellent tactician and ship handler, but I could not move the compass of his approach. Finally, I had him detached from the ship and sent to another position ashore, thinking perhaps another leader could get better results. Ultimately, I learned he failed in his career and never ascended to command.

On another occasion in the same destroyer, I worked with one of the most impressive officers I've ever met, an African American. I'll never forget his steady, calm demeanor and willingness to work with his team from the deck plates to the bridge to the combat information center. Watching him interact with his shipmates raised my spirits. I thought of the racism and bigotry he must have encountered, and how the strains of the 1930s were still part of our nation half a century later in the 1990s. We talked about the book several times, and he helped me understand it more fully.

After he'd been on board for a year, I said to him, "Vince, I want to transfer you off the ship." He was shocked, but I quickly added, "I don't have anything left to teach you. You're a better ship handler than me or the executive officer, a smarter and quicker tactician in combat, and your people adore you. You need to go on to command now." While I was sad to see him leave the ship, he was given command of a small swift patrol craft in the Arabian Gulf, and he went on from there to a highly successful career, including his own destroyer command. We remain in touch today, many years later.

To Kill a Mockingbird is a powerful and unforgettable book about race in America; the nation's flawed judicial system; and a young girl's coming of age. At times it seems to have been taken directly from the headlines of George Floyd's extrajudicial killing, the unfulfilled "Me Too" movement, or the many unequal trials we learn about almost daily. But for me, *To Kill a Mockingbird* is above all a story of mentorship, of building the next generation that will follow behind us and hopefully create a better world. I've succeeded at times in that regard and failed at others, but where I have been most successful, it has been with the steady voice of Atticus Finch whispering in my ear.

CHAPTER FIFTEEN

KNOW THE BORDERS

Catch-22

by Joseph Heller

What is a country? A country is a piece of land surrounded on all sides by boundaries, usually unnatural. Englishmen are dying for England, Americans are dying for America, Germans are dying for Germany, Russians are dying for Russia. There are now fifty or sixty countries fighting in this war. Surely so many countries can't all be worth dying for.

Catch-22 is a tragic, funny, bawdy, complex novel about an Army Air Corps unit stationed on an island in the Mediterranean Sea at the height of World War II. A cult classic of the rebellious 1960s and 1970s, it is a stunning indictment of the fundamental idiocy of war as seen through a vast cast of characters centered on protagonist and antihero Capt. John Yossarian, the bombardier on a B-25.

The book has nearly fifty distinctive characters. Told through a variety of viewpoints, it follows the exploits and misdeeds of a U.S. Army squadron engaged in highly dangerous bombing missions. Yossarian provides the moral compass of the book, which is loosely based on Heller's own experiences in the war. Yossarian is suffering from what we would recognize as PTSD today. He becomes deeply suspicious of the chain of command and the military medical establishment associated with it, and for good reason. Each time he nears the number of combat missions crews must fly to earn a ticket home, the brass raises it. By the end of the novel he has flown more than seventy. Along the way, most of his friends are killed in combat, and the corruption and venality of the U.S. military logistic system and the full horrors of war are gradually introduced to the reader. As the book ends, one of Yossarian's closest friends has finally succeeded in making his way to Sweden and we learn that Yossarian hopes to follow him there.

"Insanity is contagious."

I have read the novel twice. The first time I was a teenager and the war in Vietnam was at its height. This was in 1972 as I was preparing to head off to Annapolis, about to join the U.S. military at perhaps the lowest point in the long history of America's relationship with its armed forces. *Catch-22* is the ultimate modern antiwar novel, full of black humor designed to underscore the absurdity of war as primal and foolish. When I finished it in the months before donning a uniform for the first time, I was truly shaken by the book's bitter message: in the end, your chain of command cares not a whit for you, the causes for which you fight are unjust and nonsensical, and your mission should not be military victory but rather avoiding war itself. I almost pulled my appointment to the U.S. Naval Academy, but after long talks with my father—a recently retired Marine Corps colonel who had fought in Korea and later commanded a battalion in Vietnam—I stayed the course and took the first steps to nearly forty years in uniform.

In those long years, I saw my share of wars—Desert Storm in the first Persian Gulf conflict, the long twilight of the Cold War, skirmishes off Haiti and the Balkans, and then the nightmare of the "forever wars" in Iraq and Afghanistan—wars fought at times for causes that did not turn out to be what we envisioned or always end the way we wanted. Along the way, I saw the point Heller was making about relationships in war and how they have an intensity that can change people's perceptions of each other. As Yossarian says about a new arrival, "The Texan turned out to be good-natured, generous and likeable. In three days, no one could stand him." And there were times when my chain of command did seem more interested in their own promotion trajectory than the well-being of my Sailors. But even though there were moments when all I could do was laugh inwardly at the nonsense coming down the chain of command, they were the exceptions. Mostly, I found the men and women of my Navy to be honorable, patriotic, and deeply concerned about the Sailors entrusted to them. As I moved up through the ranks and became "the brass," I often thought of the funny, sad, and ultimately tragic messages of *Catch-22* and reminded myself that I must avoid becoming a Colonel Cathcart, the ambitious villain of the piece who is obsessed with obtaining the star of a brigadier general.

The second time I read the novel was just after I retired from active duty. It was in the summer of 2013, and I had accepted a job as dean of the Fletcher School of Law and Diplomacy at Tufts University. It seemed a good time to spend another day or so with Joseph Heller and reflect on the four decades I'd spent wearing the cloth of my nation. Had all that I had seen and learned and felt been dark? I was freshly back from my last job as Supreme Allied Commander of NATO in Europe and spending a month or so on a beach in northeast Florida with a stack of books, most of which are mentioned in this book. *Catch-22* was at the bottom of the stack because I was literally afraid to read it again. How would the military now appear to me after so many years as a part of it? Would this piercing novel have the same wounding effect it had on the young and impressionable almost-midshipman Stavridis in the spring of 1972?

On that second reading I discovered a powerful and heartfelt novel with piercing grace notes that shined a light on the admittedly absurd qualities of war, the occasional brutality of airmen and soldiers in combat, the sometimes uncaring chain of command, and the irony present in all our lives. As I had been as a teenager, I was most struck by the actual "catch" at the center of the novel.

> There was only one catch and that was Catch-22, which specified that a concern for one's safety in the face of dangers that were real and immediate was the process of a rational mind. Orr was crazy and could be grounded. All he had to do was ask; and as soon as he did, he would no longer be crazy and would have to fly more missions. Orr would be crazy to fly more missions and sane if he didn't, but if he was sane he had to fly them. If he flew them he was crazy and didn't have to; but if he didn't want to he was sane and had to. Yossarian was moved very deeply by the absolute simplicity of this clause of Catch-22 and let out a respectful whistle. "That's some catch, that Catch-22," he observed.
>
> "It's the best there is," Doc Daneeka agreed.

With that paradoxical message Joseph Heller entered the Pantheon of modern authors. But what I realized as I read the novel for a second time, now in my fifties, was that it is about much more than war. What Heller suggested to me is that in many ways our lives are grounded in absurdity and bordered by some version of the catch. In effect, we face the catch all our lives, because we know that at the end of striving through the challenges of each day, achieving what we can, caring about what seems to deeply matter, winning and losing our small battles—at the end of the struggle, we will die, passing on to whatever comes next. The small or great pile of achievements, our loves and hatreds, the sum of all we have become simply concludes, at least for us. There is no way out. As Voltaire said, in a phrase I use often as a toast to end a night with friends, "Life is a shipwreck—save what you can."

I realized on that second reading, and I know today, that *Catch-22* is really about perspective. It tells us to laugh at the foibles of life. Yes, it says, war is terrible, but so are the humans who are the enablers; and yet they are, in the end, each of us. I believe there is plenty of Yossarian in all of us, and some Cathcart as well. We are a balance of light and dark, and as Shakespeare says in *The Tempest*, putting the words in the mouth of Prospero:

> Our revels now are ended. These our actors,
> As I foretold you, were all spirits and
> Are melted into air, into thin air:
> And, like the baseless fabric of this vision,
> The cloud-capp'd towers, the gorgeous palaces,
> The solemn temples, the great globe itself,
> Ye all which it inherit, shall dissolve
> And, like this insubstantial pageant faded,
> Leave not a rack behind. We are such stuff

As dreams are made on, and our little life
Is rounded with a sleep.

In my first reading of *Catch-22* I found a cautionary tale about war. In the second reading, forty years later, I found a novel about life itself—in all its absurdity, beauty, desirability, and complexity. The book helped me put those forty years of what the British call "active service" into perspective, to frame them within the longer throw of my life, and to realize that there is always—always—a catch. We have to understand the borders and boundaries of the deal we have with life itself. This marvelous and dark novel helps us understand and accept that harsh but fundamental bargain.

CHAPTER SIXTEEN

DEAL WITH LOSS
Beloved
by Toni Morrison

Hear me now, love your heart. For this is the prize.

This is a very difficult book to read because of the challenging issues of tragedy, loss, and race in America that lie at its heart. It received the Pulitzer Prize in 1988, was a finalist for the National Book Award, and has consistently appeared on multiple lists of the best American novels of the twentieth century and of all time.

First published in 1987 by future Nobel Prize–winning author Toni Morrison, the book is set in the tumultuous years immediately after the American Civil War. The narrative follows the lives of a riven family of former slaves who have cast up near Cincinnati, Ohio, in a seemingly haunted house. It is loosely based on the true story of Margaret Garner, a woman who escaped slavery in Kentucky and fled to Ohio. When U.S. marshals broke into her home to capture her and return her to Kentucky, she attempted to kill her own children to prevent them from becoming slaves, and succeeded in killing her youngest daughter.

Morrison takes that terrible story and weaves into it a heartbreaking tale with an indelible cast of characters. At the center of the narrative are the former slave Sethe and her eighteen-year-old daughter Denver, who inhabit a house haunted by the spirit of Sethe's eldest daughter, whom she had killed to prevent her becoming a slave.

> **"Freeing yourself was one thing, claiming ownership of that freed self was another."**

After an attempted exorcism of the house fails, a young woman calling herself Beloved suddenly enters Sethe and Denver's lives. Beloved quickly becomes the central focus of the family. Tension builds between Beloved and Paul D, the former enslaved man who, like Sethe, had escaped from the plantation ironically named Sweet Home. Eventually Paul D and Beloved forge their own sexual relationship.

Sethe then reveals to Paul D the true horror of her life: when horsemen came to recapture Sethe and her children, she was forced to flee to the woods, where she killed one of her daughters. She believes that Beloved is that daughter returned to life. Sethe had insufficient money to have more than a single word engraved on the tombstone of her daughter, so she chose the word "Beloved." Sethe becomes obsessed with the "returned" daughter and gives Beloved all her attention and money.

Sethe's other daughter, Denver, comes to fear both Beloved and Sethe. Denver attempts to connect with the larger Black community but realizes that her entire family has become isolated by the nightmare of the infanticide. The ending of the novel becomes a sequence of imaginary and magical thoughts. After several confused incidents, Beloved disappears. Over time, memories of all the participants shift until the memory of Beloved is simply gone.

The novel has been controversial since its publication and has been banned in some U.S. school systems due to its depictions of slavery, infanticide, gang rape, frequent sexual encounters (many of them forced), and systemic violence. It became an issue in the 2021 governor's election in Virginia when one former governor, referring to the attempt to ban the book there, said, "I don't think parents should be telling schools what they should teach." His opponent seized on his remark and highlighted it in several commercials, which ultimately had a significant impact on the election. *Beloved* was made into a critically praised film starring Oprah Winfrey in 1998, although it struggled at the box office.

I read the book for the first time in the fall of 1995, when I was in my mid-thirties and the captain of a guided-missile destroyer. At the time, the United States was spellbound by the "trial of the century," the trial of former football star and actor O. J. Simpson for the murder of his beautiful (white) wife. The trial, which ran for an astounding eleven months, from the fall of 1994 until early October 1995, occurred just a couple of years after the Los Angeles riots of 1992, which were a reaction to brutality by the Los Angeles Police Department. Anger that had been simmering in the Los Angeles African American community for decades exploded after the brutal beating of an unarmed Black man, Rodney King, was filmed and publicized in 1991.

As I watched all the racial unrest in the country, I realized that my own understanding of race in America was sadly deficient. Certainly, I knew the basics of the introduction of slavery on these shores and our long national nightmare, finally ending the practice with the American Civil War. I'd read a few books of history of the Civil War and understood the Jim Crow era and the continuing struggles of the African American community in very general terms. I'd watched the civil rights movement press the nation forward in the late 1960s and 1970s as a teenager and college student at Annapolis.

But I didn't truly understand the history, culture, and meaning of being Black in America. I felt it most keenly when the verdict in the O. J. trial was announced and saw how the majority of my crew—mostly white—were shocked at the acquittal, while my Black crewmembers were for the most part quietly pleased. Leaving aside the merits or deficiencies of the judicial ruling, I wanted to understand the sense of history that threaded through race in America.

I began reading books that I thought could help me, including classic novels like *To Kill a Mockingbird*; *Uncle Tom's Cabin*; *The Confessions of Nat Turner*; *Absalom, Absalom!*; and *Roots*. I also began talking about race with Black fellow Navy officers. Other recommendations followed, including *Invisible Man*, *The Autobiography of Miss Jane Pittman*, and many others. Because I grew up as a competitive tennis player, I was deeply impressed by Arthur Ashe and read his autobiography, *Days of Grace*.

Beloved came up often in my conversations with African Americans. It always seemed to come with a warning that its themes of the immense pain of slavery; the terrible choices that sometimes were made, including the horror of infanticide; the importance of matriarchal power in the Black community; and the book's at times confusing magical thinking and opaque portrayal of the spirit Beloved were "not for everyone." Again and again, I heard that phrase, until I knew that I had not only to read the novel but to truly study it, the way I had heretofore delved into the classics of my own Greek heritage and my profession (Homer's epics and the classic sea novels).

And so I came to *Beloved*. I read it over the course of a week in my captain's chair on a destroyer on the choppy seas off the Virginia coast. Even now, almost thirty years later, I can remember the rough seas, gloomy skies, and rain squalls of the rolling Atlantic Ocean. And I would look up from the book, stare at the sea, and think about slavery and all its attendant horrors, and above all about the horrors of the slave ships that upended forever the lives of Africans and brought them in a nightmarish voyage to America's shores. No other novel has ever so fully absorbed me and pulled me into its unique rhythms, language, and messages—and at the same time repelled me with its unceasingly harsh events. I have read most of the books that are important to me at least twice, and many of them three or four times. I've read Voltaire's satiric masterpiece of hope, *Candide*, more than ten times. But I've never found the courage to pick up *Beloved* for another reading; it is too painful a story to return to.

I ask myself today, thirty years on, what did I take away from *Beloved*? Did reading and truly studying this novel help me be a better leader, a more empathetic person?

First, as a white man who has benefited from my own privilege, I found the book a visceral and at times stunning wake-up call. Some things are too terrible to look at straight on; you need to sidle up to them and gradually turn your gaze until you can comprehend them. The slavery that was practiced in the United States for centuries was such a horror. *Beloved* helped me begin to understand that long tragedy, tendrils of which still haunt our society.

The book is also, most immediately, about resilience. Sethe is a survivor, a woman who had inflicted upon her the very worst humans have to offer. Yet she resists, again and again: engineering her escape, fighting back hard at every turn, and taking the hardest decision any parent would ever contemplate in killing her own daughter. What *Beloved* says to me is that there are some moments in our lives when there is literally no way out, and then you must make the hard choice. But what you cannot do is simply collapse on the floor sobbing and give up.

And finally, the novel is about all the challenges of families. Mother-daughter relationships of course are at the center of the narrative, but Toni Morrison also interrogates the role of men in these deeply difficult situations. Through the characters of Paul D and Stamp Paid we see the impossible choices that men face alongside the even harder ones of women. Which is to say that yes, family relationships are hard, unstable, and often unrelentingly difficult. But they are necessary and central to who we are in the end.

All of this is packaged in beautiful prose that captures the individual spirits of the protagonists. Over time, as readers, we become deeply attached to them. By the novel's end we are still uncertain who Beloved really was—a flesh-and-blood woman pretending to be a slain daughter; a spirit made flesh, seeking closure with the mother who took her life; or a figment of Sethe's imagination. Different readers will make different interpretations, but what cannot be ignored is the power of Morrison's prose and the constant and tragic essence of her message.

Loss affects each of us in different ways, but whatever the loss and whoever we are, we must face even the greatest heartaches with courage and resilience. When I read *Beloved* so many years ago, I marveled at the courage of the author to tell this fraught story, but even more so at the extraordinary power of her message of resilience. *Listen,* Toni Morrison said to me on the pages of this stunning novel, *there are horrors in our history. Don't you dare look away.*

CHAPTER SEVENTEEN

UNDERSTAND THE PROCESS

The Caine Mutiny
by Herman Wouk

> Captain, I'm sorry, but you're a sick man.
> I'm relieving you as captain of this ship
> under Article One Eighty-Four.

This powerful novel opens during World War II with the arrival of an impressionable young ensign, Willie Keith, to serve in the dilapidated minesweeper USS *Caine*. A Princeton graduate, Willie is impressed by the ship's executive officer (second in command), Steve Maryk, a seasoned sailor; and the communications officer, slippery would-be novelist Tom Keefer. The three men become close when a new commanding officer, Lieutenant Commander Queeg arrives to take charge.

A strict disciplinarian, Queeg institutes a harsh regime. He frequently loses his temper and berates the officers and crew. He is also an incompetent seaman. During a gunnery exercise he cuts the tow line of the target *Caine* is pulling for target practice and then attempts to cover up his mistake. Soon the ship is ordered to leave Pearl Harbor to escort a group of smaller craft conducting a landing on an island in the Pacific. During this important mission, Queeg demonstrates cowardice by turning the ship away and leaving the escorted ships to do the best they can in the face of enemy fire.

> "Well, he's certainly Navy."
> "Yeah. So was Captain Bligh."

Queeg's demeanor troubles the wardroom, and Tom Keefer encourages the second in command, Maryk, to relieve the captain based on Navy Regulations as mentally unfit to command. Maryk rejects the idea, which he sees as a path to mutiny, but starts keeping a logbook to document the captain's failures and disturbing behaviors. A further incident involving some missing strawberries seems to show a mentally deteriorating and paranoid Captain Queeg.

Events come to a frightening head during a typhoon when the ship appears to be in danger of foundering. Under extreme pressure, Maryk takes the extraordinary step of relieving Queeg of command under Article 184 of Navy Regulations. Maryk returns the ship to San Francisco, where both he and Willie are charged with mutiny and forced to face a court-martial. Lt. Barney Greenwald, a naval aviator, is appointed to defend them because he was a lawyer in civilian life, but he makes it clear he does not want the job and does not respect what Maryk and Willie did.

During the court-martial, Tom Keefer testifies that he never saw any sign of mental illness in Queeg, a deliberate and cowardly lie. But Greenwald puts Queeg on the stand and gradually brings out the captain's paranoic personality until he has a psychiatric meltdown. Willie and Maryk are acquitted, although Maryk's career is clearly over. Afterward, Greenwald, the winning attorney, comes to the wardroom and flips the narrative, slamming the wardroom for not supporting Queeg. He correctly names Tom Keefer as the real coward and throws a glass of champagne in his face, challenging him to a fight—which Keefer, true to his character—declines.

> "Situation quiet; the captain's been put away for the night."

Willie Keith returns to the *Caine* as second in command during the fierce Okinawa campaign toward the end of the war. Tom Keefer is now the captain, and he turns out to be an incompetent leader reminiscent of Queeg. The ship is hit by a kamikaze, and Willie leads the efforts to save the ship even after Keefer panics and orders the crew to abandon ship. Willie is awarded a Bronze Star for his behavior in saving the ship and eventually becomes captain of *Caine*—but, ironically, also receives a letter of reprimand for his role in the mutiny.

As the novel concludes, Will Keith has successfully brought the tired ship back to the United States; has reunited with his on-again, off-again girlfriend, May; and is on the streets during the parade celebrating victory over Japan. The book, much of it based on the author's wartime experiences, has been adapted for screen, stage, and television productions.

I've read the novel twice, and each time I took away different lessons. I've also watched the classic film starring Humphrey Bogart as Queeg. The book is much smaller in scope and scale than Herman Wouk's masterpieces, *The Winds of War* and *War and Remembrance*. Instead of the vast canvas of World War II portrayed in the two much longer books, *The Caine Mutiny* focuses narrowly on four strongly drawn characters, each of whom has a role to play in teaching the reader about life in the crucible of war at sea.

The first and most important lesson of the book is represented by Steve Maryk: the challenges of life at sea and the need for true competence as a mariner, tactician, and leader. Although Maryk is taken in by the scheming Tom Keefer and seduced into a mutiny, he still represents much of what is good about a seagoing officer. He is a fine seaman, a good shipmate, and courageous in the face of both combat and the typhoon that ultimately sets in motion the events leading him to relieve Queeg for cause. His career is destroyed because he doesn't understand the process of command, the imperative of good order and discipline, and how the system will ultimately move to protect a commander—even a deeply flawed one like Queeg.

As a junior officer I worked once for a Queeg-like captain, although the wardroom never came close to trying to relieve him. We simply bore the slings and arrows of his toxic leadership style. That was more than forty years ago, and—fortunately—things have changed in the Navy. There is far less tendency to close ranks around a terrible leader, and junior officers today are far more empowered. As I worked my way up the ranks to become a sea captain myself, I tried to be the best mariner, tactician, and leader I could be, and some of what I took away from the character of Steve Maryk contributed to that.

Perhaps equally important thematically is the fatally flawed Captain Queeg. Today we would think of him as suffering from battle fatigue or posttraumatic stress disorder. This is alluded to several times, and the attorney Greenberg highlights it when he confronts the wardroom after the court-martial. Despite Queeg's poor performance as a mariner, tactician, and leader—and his unmistakable cowardice at several points—he is a strangely sympathetic figure when viewed through Greenberg's eyes. The lessons of Captain Queeg are obvious: don't get bogged down in minutiae; be courageous in battle; be courteous and kind to your subordinates; and above all don't sully the immense honor of commanding a U.S. Navy warship, especially in combat.

The third character representing one of the book's themes is the despicable Tom Keefer, a coward who is constantly seeking to manipulate his shipmates. An aspiring novelist, he wants to keep his hands clean while improving his own position by torpedoing Queeg. He correctly sees that Maryk isn't the sharpest tool in the drawer, even if he is a fine navigator and ship handler. Keefer also sees that Willie is callow, inexperienced, and susceptible to manipulation. Keefer effectively lays a trap, draws them in, and then steps back to make sure he doesn't find himself in trouble. Unlike either Maryk or Willie, Keefer understands the process perfectly—but uses his understanding of it for his own inappropriate ends.

I've met my share of Keefers along my life voyage. Some of them were what we would call at the Naval Academy "smacks"—sycophants who tell a boss what they think he wants to hear, and thus find their way to plum jobs and advancement in the ranks. Unfortunately, there are a few Keefers at the very top of the military's food chain, four-star officers who are always keeping an eye on their own résumés, thinking about the next job in uniform or how to shape their career to find lucrative employment after retiring from active service. They are self-promoters who don't want to take the time to mentor younger officers. The Keefers are often hard to spot, but fortunately they are few in number. Officers' "service reputation" is built like a wall—a brick at a time based on all they do and how they handle themselves from the deck of a destroyer to the halls of the Pentagon to the desks of the Naval War College. Over time the truth about someone's character usually comes out, as was the case for Tom Keefer.

And finally, we have young Wille Keith. Every ship has a few Willie Keiths—junior officers who think they are way smarter than the Navy, are very critical of their seniors, and really don't know what they are doing. I certainly had some of Willie's faults in my own first tour, but I was lucky to work for a fine executive officer, Dusty Rhodes, a "mustang" who had come up through the ranks; and a brilliant captain, Fritz Gaylord. The CO and XO took the time to sand down my rough edges, helped me become a team player, reduced my arrogance to a manageable level, and sent me on to my next ship after a few years as a far better officer. What I learned through that experience was how important that first tour at sea will be for each young ensign and lieutenant, junior grade.

I tried in all my subsequent command tours to keep in mind the trajectory of Willie Keith's career and avoid becoming frustrated or short-tempered with young officers—no matter how green they seemed to be. In a word, I tried to teach them the *process* of the Navy—how the big impersonal machine can be bent to an individual's improvement; the ways a service reputation is built; why teamwork and collaboration, not cutthroat competition, are so important for each wardroom; and how we are all dependent on the shipmates with whom we serve.

And as I have moved on to new jobs after the Navy—in higher education leading a graduate school at Tufts University and today as a senior executive at the Carlyle Group, an international financial firm—all of the lessons of *The Caine Mutiny* pertain. No matter where you are, you've got to understand the process of your organization. And the odds are high that you won't be able to figure it out on your own. Finding the right people to admire and emulate, and hopefully convincing them to mentor you, is an essential life skill. I learned a fair amount of that on the deck plates of a variety of ships, some shiny and new and others beat-up old tubs like *Caine*. And I also learned it from reading this fine sea novel, so full of apt observations about the complexity of human relationships, especially in moments of real stress. Set sail on USS *Caine*, and you will very likely come away with a new and more nuanced perspective on the long voyage of your life.

CHAPTER EIGHTEEN

NEVER LOSE YOUR TEMPER

The Quiet Warrior

by *Thomas Buell*

> A man's judgment is best when he can forget himself and any reputation he may have acquired and can concentrate wholly on making the right decisions.

Most naval officers who have studied World War II agree that Fleet Admiral Chester Nimitz was the overall architect of the victory in the Pacific. Nimitz took command of the battered Pacific Fleet a few weeks after Pearl Harbor, when once mighty Battleship Row consisted of eight damaged hulks, thousands of Sailors and officers were dead, and USS *Arizona* was a tomb for more than a thousand men on the bottom of the harbor. Instead of assuming command in a grand ceremony on the deck of a spic-and-span battleship, Nimitz took up the mantle of command on the deck of a small diesel submarine, wearing working khakis instead of the traditional ceremonial service dress whites. The smell of fuel oil, cordite, and death was everywhere around him.

Standing amid the widespread destruction and despair, Nimitz chose to resolutely focus on the positives. He still had his fast carriers, which had been out of port when the attack came early on a quiet Sunday, December 7, 1941. Luckily, a handful of heavy cruisers had likewise survived. Also, the Japanese had missed the massive fuel farms at Pearl Harbor, giving Nimitz flexibility to operate his remaining ships at long range. But most important of all, Nimitz had a pair of fighting admirals at his disposal, and he moved them swiftly up the command structure to lead the counterattacks against Japan over the next several years.

One was the mercurial, inspirational, and impulsive Vice Adm. William Halsey. "Bull" Halsey was quick with a quip, colorful in his language, and utterly aggressive at sea. The other was the quiet, cerebral, and measured Rear Adm. Ray Spruance. Despite their different personalities they were close friends, and each admired the essential qualities of the other. Over the coming months, Nimitz grew to rely on both men, and eventually decided to alternate them in command of the enormous striking power of the "big blue fleet," which was designated the Third Fleet when Halsey commanded and the Fifth Fleet when under Spruance.

Naval historians and Navy officers like me have their own opinions about the two. There is a kind of informal "Team Halsey" and "Team Spruance" mentality in the conversations about them. While there are aspects of Fleet Admiral Halsey's command philosophy that I admire—notably his intense aggressive streak, which he expressed as: "Hit hard, hit fast, hit often"—but ultimately, I come down with Team Spruance. And the more I study his life, philosophy, battle strategy, and results in combat, the more certain I am that Spruance was the better flag officer. I've taken a lot of lessons from Admiral Spruance's life and career, and it is his calm, rational, thoughtful, and almost serene demeanor that I most admire. The main lesson I learned from Ray Spruance was simple and has stood me in good stead throughout my career: don't lose your temper.

This comes across again and again in Thomas Buell's superb biography of Admiral Spruance, *The Quiet Warrior*. I read it first when I was a very young officer serving, ironically, in a *Spruance*-class destroyer, USS *Hewitt*, in the late 1970s. Spruance's example helped me overcome some of the impulsiveness and uneven temperament I had in my early twenties. I picked the book up again when I went to command NATO in 2009, and finally dipped into it again in preparing this volume. Buell was highly qualified to write the book: he was a 1958 Annapolis graduate who served at sea in destroyers over his career; and his crisp, well-documented writing earned the book the Navy League's Alfred Thayer Mahan Award when it was published.

Spruance had many fine qualities, but at the top of the list was his absolutely calm temperament. In each of my commands, I've tried to maintain that kind of equilibrium, and also to insist that others do so as well. I've always tried to create an "anger free" zone wherever I've had the authority of command to do so, and I learned to do that reading this biography of Spruance. I found it particularly useful twice in my career, first in my initial destroyer command and then at NATO as Supreme Allied Commander.

USS *Barry*, my first command, set incredibly high standards for its crew and engineering. The entire crew had been hand-picked; the CO and XO, respectively, of the commissioning crew went on to be a four-star Chief of Naval Operations and a three-star vice admiral. *Barry* was the first guided missile destroyer built by Ingalls Shipyard in Mississippi, and as such received special attention from the shipyard. Given all the talent on board, there was an enormous amount of self-pressure in the wardroom, and, especially, the chiefs' mess. People tended to be short with each other and to lose their tempers when something did not go perfectly.

Using the tenets of Ray Spruance, I tried hard to take some of the tension out of the ship, and ultimately succeeded. We took the ship out on its maiden deployment, conducting missions in Haiti, the Balkans, and the Arabian Gulf. I commanded the ship for well over two years, and I hope some of what I learned about command climate and a calm leadership demeanor from Admiral Spruance became part of the legacy of *Barry*—which won the Battenberg Cup as the top ship in the Atlantic Fleet in those years.

At the far end of my career, as NATO commander, I found immense tensions bubbling through my command because of the challenges the allies faced in Afghanistan. We had 150,000 troops in active combat throughout my four years at the peak of the war. Every day, we received reports of our troops killed or grievously wounded. The cultural differences between the twenty-eight nations of the alliance and the twenty-two additional coalition partners were palpable, with finger-pointing about everything from a perceived lack of combat skills to how logistics were apportioned in-theater. It was an incredibly tense environment, which was very understandable given the situation in what truly felt like a "forever war."

As I mentioned above, I'd reread *The Quiet Warrior* before taking command of NATO in May 2009. And again, as in earlier commands, I tried very consciously to lower the temperature across the vast command. This meant endless rounds of meetings in all the national capitals; going to Afghanistan, Iraq, the Balkans, and on antipiracy missions personally and often; working with the Afghan government and irascible President Hamid Karzai and his successor, the ill-fated Ashraf Ghani; and counseling the hundreds of admirals and generals spread across the command structure. Under me I had my share of both Halseys and Spruances, along with many others who did not meet those high marks. But throughout the four years I commanded the alliance's operations, from Libya to Afghanistan to Kosovo, we worked hard to keep anger, impulse, and irrationality out of the equation—due in part to Buell's fine biography of Ray Spruance.

Spruance was born not far from the Naval Academy, in Baltimore, and graduated with the class of 1906. He was a classic surface warfare officer, serving in and commanding battleships, cruisers, and destroyers for most of his early career. Early on, he sailed in Theodore Roosevelt's Great White Fleet, which circumnavigated the globe from 1907 to 1909. Spruance commanded five destroyers and the battleship *Mississippi* before ascending to flag rank. His shore duty assignments included engineering assignments in Washington, D.C.; New York; London; and Edinburgh, Scotland. As a Greek American, I was delighted to learn he was awarded a Gold Cross by the Greek government for his service in the Aegean in the 1920s during periods of high tension between Turkey and Greece.

Spruance also found time to attend the U.S. Naval War College, which he would go on to lead as president decades later after World War II ended. By the time the Pearl Harbor attack launched the war in December 1941, he had completed his battleship command and served in his first flag officer assignment in command of the 10th Naval District in the Caribbean. As the war unfolded, he was initially in command of Cruiser Division Five with six heavy cruisers under him, attached to Vice Admiral Halsey's forces conducting targeted counterattacks throughout the western Pacific and launching the Doolittle raid on Japan itself.

By May 1942 it was clear that the Japanese were planning another significant attack. Intelligence code-crackers were able to narrow the target down to the Midway atoll, 1,300 miles across the Pacific from Hawaii. The Japanese leaders believed that a strike on Midway would further threaten the United States and Hawaii, and perhaps induce the United States to negotiate a peace. Nimitz decided to counter the Japanese with his carrier force under Vice Admiral Halsey. But Halsey came down with a vicious rash, possibly shingles, and was unable to maintain command. Enter Ray Spruance, who at that point had zero experience commanding carriers in combat, although he had been an integral part of Halsey's forces as a cruiser commander. Spruance sailed toward Midway with the carriers *Enterprise*, *Yorktown*, and *Hornet*.

The American ships were facing a strong Japanese force that included four carriers, but Spruance correctly calculated that Midway itself would function essentially as an unsinkable aircraft carrier for whichever force controlled it. And he had the element of surprise bestowed by the cryptographers back at Pearl Harbor. The Japanese had no idea that the U.S. force was headed their way. The U.S. Navy won the most important single battle in its history at Midway, sinking all four Japanese carriers while losing only the gallant *Yorktown*, which had been hurriedly patched up following heavy damage in recent combat.

For my money, it was Spruance's calm, methodical approach that won the day. His subordinates sometimes talked of Spruance's "electric brain," and he was known for keeping quiet, constantly thinking through the odds for any given action, often while walking around his carrier's decks and flag bridge. While some have criticized him for not pursuing the retreating Japanese surface forces more aggressively, my sense is that he knew full well that the essence of the victory was the destruction of the Japanese carriers—and even more important, their well-trained and experienced pilots. He measured the odds at the end of the battle and decided to take the major victory and not risk his carriers against the Japanese heavy surface battleships and cruisers that he knew were lying in wait. Recognizing the sweep of the victory, Fleet Admiral Nimitz moved to make Spruance first his chief of staff, and then deputy commander of the entire Pacific Fleet.

From 1943 onward, Nimitz alternated Spruance and Halsey in command. The Sailors loved the bold, quotable Halsey; but the subordinate commanders preferred the predictable, thoughtful, and calm Spruance. A cruiser captain who served under both admirals later said, "My feeling was one of confidence when Spruance was there." Spruance went on to win significant battles off Saipan in the Battle of the Philippine Sea, while the impulsive Halsey almost lost the pivotal Battle of Leyte Gulf. Buell quotes Spruance as saying of the Battle of the Philippine Sea, "As a matter of tactics I think that going out after the Japanese and knocking their carriers out would have been much better and more satisfactory than waiting for them to attack us, but we were at the start of a very important and large amphibious operation and we could not afford to gamble and place it in jeopardy."

> "So far as my getting five-star rank is concerned, if I could have got it along with Bill Halsey, that would have been fine; but, if I had received it instead of Bill Halsey, I would have been very unhappy over it."

A true measure of his humility came as the war ended. Congress decided to make four Fleet Admirals, giving them five-star rank. Those chosen were Leahy, King, Nimitz, . . . and Halsey. Many of Spruance's supporters were disappointed, but Ray Spruance himself—a close friend of Halsey—never said an unkind word about it. He went on to be a U.S. ambassador to the Philippines in the 1950s, served with distinction as president of the Naval War College, and received multiple honorary degrees. Throughout his life, he was a habitual long-distance walker, a nonsmoker in a time and culture where everyone lit up a cigarette at the start of every meeting, and a passionate gardener.

He is buried alongside three of his fellow Pacific war admirals and their wives—Chester Nimitz, Richmond Turner, and Charles Lockwood. These four giants of the twentieth-century Navy sail on together in the Golden Gate National Cemetery just outside of San Francisco, with a good view out over the vast Pacific that was their battlefield. That 1970s *Spruance*-class destroyer that I served on four decades ago is long gone now, but a brand-new *Arleigh Burke*–class guided missile destroyer named for Ray Spruance has taken its place. I hope there will always be a USS *Spruance* in the Navy as a tribute to a superb combat leader, a fine shipmate to his fellow naval officers, and a guiding light in the world of calm, thoughtful leadership.

CHAPTER NINETEEN

DELEGATE FREELY

Nimitz at War

by Craig Symonds

Some of the best advice I've had comes from junior officers and enlisted men.

—Fleet Admiral Chester W. Nimitz

When I was a seventeen-year-old midshipman newly arrived at Annapolis, my favorite course was "Sea Power." I was lucky to be in the section of about twenty plebes taught by the grand old professor of maritime history, E. B. Potter. Professor Potter had a brilliant career as a naval historian and produced narrative histories of World War II as well as a handful of biographies of the war's great admirals: Arleigh Burke, the swashbuckling destroyer captain; William "Bull" Halsey, the flamboyant aviator and carrier commander; and the serene commander of the Pacific Fleet, Chester Nimitz.

He knew them all personally, and in some ways, I think, loved them equally. But late in the second semester of the course, after nearly a year studying the entire pantheon of combat admirals—from the ancient Greek Themistocles of Salamis to Vice Admiral Lord Nelson of Trafalgar to the American modern admiralty—we asked him to name the best of them all. I despise the sports term "Greatest of All Time," or GOAT, because it is unfair to decide among the variables of time, place, competition, and outcome. Could Lord Nelson have won at Midway, as Spruance did? Or could Halsey have triumphed at Trafalgar or Salamis? We'll never know, and thus such comparisons are all ephemeral, like trying to predict whether Rod Laver could have defeated Roger Federer or Novak Djokovic.

But in that spring moment in an Annapolis classroom, there was clearly no doubt in the mind of our professor, who had studied the men's careers exhaustively, from the battlefields of the sea to the halls of the Pentagon. He looked out the window, smiled, and said, "Nimitz. He was the best of them all." Then he discarded the lesson plan for the day and spent the hour telling us about Chester W. Nimitz. It turned out that the first edition of Potter's best-selling book, *Sea Power*, had been cowritten with Fleet Admiral Nimitz. Later editions, which Potter solely edited and wrote, became the very textbook we were using. It was a moving and heartfelt impromptu paean, a song of praise to a man Professor Potter not only revered but loved.

And that was the beginning of my forty-year-long study of the life of Nimitz. During my four years at the U.S. Naval Academy I often walked past Nimitz Hall, the largest academic building on campus and the library. Every night, seeking to get out of my crowded dormitory of Bancroft Hall, I would walk across the campus and set up to study in a quiet corner of the library. Newly opened in that same spring of 1973, Nimitz Hall has for fifty years been the academic anchor of the Academy.

In January 1976, my graduation year, Professor Potter published his remarkable and personal biography of Fleet Admiral Nimitz. I was able to attend the book launch just a few months before my own launch into the fleet as an officer of the surface line. My days at Annapolis were intertwined with the history of Fleet Admiral Nimitz in every sense, and I often felt I was sailing in his wake.

So, as I prepared this list of twenty-five books that helped me in my own career and life, I knew that I needed a volume that highlighted the life of Nimitz. My initial instinct, of course, was to select Professor Potter's biography, and I almost did. But a couple of years ago, a professor closer to my own age, Craig Symonds, published what I consider an even better portrait of Fleet Admiral Nimitz. A Naval Reservist and distinguished maritime historian, Dr. Symonds wrote his Ph.D. dissertation in 1976 on the early history of naval policy in the United States. He succeeded Professor Potter—talk about large shoes to fill—as the top specialist in naval history and served as chair of the History Department until retiring in 2005. He later taught at the Naval War College as well.

In 2022, he published his twenty-first book, *Nimitz at War: Leadership from Pearl Harbor to Tokyo Bay*, bringing a lifetime of study and analysis of leadership in maritime combat to examine in striking depth the personal leadership of Chester Nimitz. I've read it twice, and each time I put it down I felt a pang of regret to be leaving the company of Fleet Admiral Nimitz. As I read, I had a palpable sense of sailing alongside Nimitz from the shattering opening days of the war to the ultimate triumph of the Pacific Fleet over a powerful and relentless foe. With all due respect to

E. B. Potter, this version of Nimitz' life is the better book and thus lands on this list.

While Potter's rendering gives a more sweeping view of Nimitz, Symonds distills the Nimitz touch. Many naval historians have written about "the Nelson touch," referring to the leadership style of Vice Admiral Horatio Nelson. But the Nimitz touch displayed in World War II in the Pacific is a better guide to the most important elements of leadership. I think the Nimitz touch consists of three essential elements: innovation, resilience, and humility. But it is the element that underlies and supports those three core principles that I see as most influential in the life of Nimitz: the willingness to delegate. In many ways it is the most difficult trait to master, especially for personally talented leaders.

> "Leadership consists of picking good men and helping them do their best."

The grandson of a Texas Ranger, Nimitz was born in Fredericksburg, Texas, where the National Museum of the Pacific War is now located—ironically far from the ocean. His father died before he was born, and the young Nimitz was influenced by his grandfathers, one a Texan and the other a German merchant seaman. It is no surprise, then, that Nimitz attended the U.S. Naval Academy. He was a distinguished graduate of the class of 1905, in the top 10 percent of his class. His early career as a destroyer officer was marred when he ran aground his first command, USS *Decatur*, just three years after leaving Annapolis. While he received a letter of reprimand, his exceptional talent allowed him to overcome that early misstep—an initial indication of the remarkable resilience of the man who would become one of America's first Fleet Admirals.

He moved on to the realm of submarines, which at that time were at the cutting edge of the world's navies, assuming command of a series of the early gasoline-powered boats. Always an innovator, he was at the forefront of design changes that led to the construction of far safer diesel-powered submarines. In another example of innovation, Nimitz helped pioneer the concept of underway refueling and rearming of ships at sea in the 1920s. He went on in the interwar period to command cruisers and submarines in both the Pacific and Atlantic fleets, always pushing the envelope in terms of their operational employment. After World War II, when he was the Chief of Naval Operations, he undertook perhaps the greatest (and highest-risk) procurement program in naval history: the creation of nuclear-powered submarines. Without Fleet Admiral Nimitz at the helm of the Navy, the brilliant Adm. Hyman Rickover—the father of nuclear power at sea—would never have succeeded. In terms of innovation, Nimitz often said, "If you're not making waves, you're not under weigh." When I was a destroyer captain for the first time, I had that saying embossed on a plaque that I kept on the door to my sea cabin as a reminder to my wardroom of the need to grasp new ideas.

Immediately after Pearl Harbor, two-star Rear Adm. Chester Nimitz was tapped for a direct promotion to four stars and command of the shattered Pacific Fleet. As he stood on the deck of one of his beloved submarines, USS *Grayling*, and took command of the broken fleet, he squared his shoulders and demonstrated the second quality that marked him throughout his life and career: resilience. He was quick to focus the fleet on its remaining advantages: the fast carriers, submarines, and superb code-breakers. What we see in *Nimitz at War* is a man of relentless optimism, but not a Pollyanna-like cheerleader. His was a quiet, thoughtful style of leadership grounded in a sure knowledge of what was right and driven to grind through obstacles. "When you're in command, command," he often told his officers, reminiscent of Napoleon's nineteenth-century dictum, "If you set out to take Vienna, take Vienna." All great commanders in history, at sea or ashore, shared the qualities of resiliency and iron-willed determination.

Throughout the long years of the Pacific War, Nimitz was surrounded by men of vast ego. His peer commander, Army general Douglas MacArthur, fancied himself the greatest warrior of the ages, and let everyone know it. Adm. William "Bull" Halsey never saw a microphone he wouldn't seize to trumpet his own triumphs; and Nimitz's boss, Fleet Admiral Ernest King, went so far as to design a new style of uniforms for the entire Navy (which largely ignored them unless he was around). Of all the four-star officers in command throughout the war, Nimitz had the highest level not of ego but of humility. He constantly sought advice from others and was generous in acknowledging their contributions. He often said, with utter sincerity, that the best advice he received came from enlisted Sailors and junior officers. Throughout his long life he was known as a loyal shipmate and friend to seniors, peers, and subordinates. And that humility was a fundamental key to his success.

But as I reflected on the lessons I could take from Fleet Admiral Nimitz in reading *Nimitz at War*, what really stood out was his peerless ability to delegate. He was a master at the three essential steps of delegation. First, you must be able to pick the right people, weighing their attributes and abilities without prejudice and then making what can be tough choices.

In my seven years as a four-star commander, both at U.S. Southern Command and then as Supreme Allied Commander of NATO, I spent at least a fourth of my time choosing the right people. Sometimes I failed and brought someone to a senior post for which they turned out to be unready; but for the most part I was able to find and advance the right people for the right jobs. When I needed a deputy at U.S. European Command, I turned to Lt. Gen. Jack Gardner, a West Point graduate and peer. His calm, thoughtful leadership as deputy commander while I was so completely occupied on the NATO side of my responsibilities was noteworthy. He was followed by Vice Adm. Charlie Martoglio, who had been my second in command on my first at-sea command, USS *Barry*. A visionary destroyer officer, Charlie brought innovation and a dynamic command style to Europe exactly as I'd hoped he would. In both men I found leaders I could completely trust to make the hardest decisions, from the storage and protection of nuclear weapons to relations with our Israeli partners.

The second crucial part of delegation I learned from the career of Fleet Admiral Nimitz is to simply let go. There is no point in spending a great deal of time selecting people for subordinate positions and then micromanaging their efforts. I learned that at U.S. Southern Command, when my initial inclination was to sit too firmly on top of my superbly talented team, thinking—with my own ego engaged—that I was the ultimate source of good ideas. When I turned over important decisions to leaders like Rear Adm. Harry Harris, the operations officer, while I focused on counternarcotics, things tended to work out better in Colombia. The entire idea of delegation is to give up minute-to-minute management of a problem. Ultimately this benefits the larger organization, not only generally, with better outcomes, but also by preparing subordinates for later command opportunities. Rear Admiral Harris, for example, went on to a brilliant career and became a four-star himself in command of the vast Indo-Pacific Command, and served as U.S. ambassador in Seoul, Korea, after retiring from the Navy.

Third, and finally, a key part of delegation—after selection and empowerment—is to quietly monitor the tasks *without interfering*. In some ways this is the hardest part, of course. As I watched Rear Admiral Harris work closely with our partners in Colombia, I naturally had my own ideas about good missions and targets in the fight against a virulent insurgency of Marxist guerrillas, the FARC. While I was content that Harris was doing all that was needed and necessary, I also realized that part of my command responsibility was to provide some oversight and top cover. In my daily intelligence briefings, I always had a special report on operations in Colombia, and also kept open my independent channels of communications with our ambassadors in Bogotá, who were deeply involved in the challenges. The art of delegation is knowing when to lean in with a quiet suggestion, and when to really take control.

By the time I was a four-star, I had finally figured that out, but I had plenty of missteps along the way. When I was a young destroyer captain trying to let my junior officers learn how to really handle *Barry*, I found myself occasionally letting them go too far in driving the ship. Once, in Baltimore Harbor, I allowed a young ensign to stay in control of the ship just a minute or two longer than was advisable, and she put a sizable dent in the stern of the ship on a concrete pier. A friend of mine in a nearby cruiser saw the dent later that day and asked about it. When I explained, "I just let the ensign go too far," he said, "Well, *Captain*, that's why we put you on the ship. To make sure you don't over-delegate at the wrong moment. But a little paint should fix that, and they can hammer it out back in Norfolk."

When I look at Nimitz in his senior commands, I see a master class in knowing the moment when monitoring must change to taking the helm. Perhaps a comparative instance for Nimitz came when then–Vice Admiral Halsey came down with shingles in the run-up to Midway and, despite his protests, had to be removed from command of the carriers. Nimitz knew when to take charge. He put Rear Admiral Spruance in command, and Spruance won the crucial battle of Midway. Nimitz afterward alternated them—sort of paired delegation—in command of the Pacific Fleet until the successful conclusion of the war.

For those seeking to understand Nimitz's eventful and commendable life alongside the leadership techniques that energized it, I offer two suggestions. One is to make the pilgrimage to the Museum of the Pacific in Fredericksburg, Texas, where you can commune with Nimitz' spirit and literally feel his presence in the Texas hill country. And the other is simply to pick up a copy of Professor Symonds' brilliant biography, which will transport you to the hard, hard days of World War II and illustrate the sterling character of the greatest admiral in history. It really is Chester Nimitz.

Godspeed and open water wherever you sail today, sir.

CHAPTER TWENTY

NEVER OBSESS

All the Pretty Horses
by Cormac McCarthy

Scared money can't win, and a
worried man can't love.

Published in 1992, *All the Pretty Horses* is a masterful novel of the twentieth-century American West written in lean, understated prose. I first read it during Operation Desert Shield/Desert Storm when I was in the war zone of the Arabian Gulf and second in command of a new *Ticonderoga*-class guided missile destroyer. It had been on my radar after it won the National Book Award, and I'd read and loved several of Cormac McCarthy's previous novels, including the iconic *Blood Meridian*. I remember describing *Pretty Horses* to my wife, Laura, in one of the letters I sent her daily as our forces prepared to attack Saddam Hussein's forces during their illegal occupation of

Kuwait. It was hard to describe exactly why the story struck me so profoundly, particularly as its setting—West Texas and Mexico in the late 1940s—was so utterly different from the flat, hot gulf waters around me.

Looking back, I suppose that is the novel's power: it completely transports the reader into another time and place, touches on the big themes of life, and, hopefully, teaches us a bit about our own voyage in the world. I would come down from the bridge, where I spent long hours each day (the captain and I alternated being on the bridge or down in the combat information center in case of incoming missiles), and eagerly pick up the book for an hour before grabbing a bit of sleep.

Each page pulled me thousands of miles away to 1949 Texas and into the life and times of sixteen-year-old cowboy John Grady Cole. The teenager has a series of adventures south of the American border that revolve around horses, lawbreakers, and the "code of the West." It is an almost picaresque novel (*Don Quixote* appears in it) that takes the reader deep into the mind of the protagonist and his laconic, balanced, and stable approach to the turmoil that confronts him and his companions. The primary message for me was simple: stay calm and keep things in perspective, no matter how difficult the voyage becomes. In essence, *Pretty Horses* tells us that "the world is a big dangerous place, bad things are going to happen, and all you can do is try your best and keep your honor." That message—avoid the human tendency to obsess about things we can't control—is a pretty good one, especially for those in a war zone thousands of miles from family and friends.

> **"My daddy used to tell me not to chew on something that was eating you."**

Stylistically, McCarthy was influenced somewhat by Ernest Hemingway. Both authors have an ear for dialogue that sounds truly genuine. McCarthy's choice to eschew the use of quotation marks to set apart dialogue further contributes to the book's sense of spare realism. We are introduced to John Grady Cole as he comes of age on a ranch owned by his grandfather and worked by Mexicans. As a result of his interactions with the Mexicans he is bilingual, and parts of the novel are in Spanish without the benefit of translation. I speak Spanish today (thanks to years in Latin America as commander of U.S. Southern Command) but was far from fluent the first time I read the book. I found—and I suspect other non-Spanish-speaking readers will find—that the context makes these passages clear.

As the story begins, Grady is facing a big life change: his grandfather died, and the ranch is going to be sold. He doesn't want to relocate into town, so he and his best friend, Lacey Rawlins, head south across the porous U.S.-Mexican border to find a working ranch where they can hook on as cowboys. On the way they encounter a young cowboy named Jimmy Blevins, who has a sketchy story and a valuable horse that is clearly stolen. From the moment he arrives on the scene, Blevins creates trouble for the two young Texans. He promptly loses both his beautiful horse and a vintage Colt pistol and inveigles Grady and Rawlins to come with him into a nearby Mexican town to try and recover them. This turns out badly for Blevins, but eventually Grady and Rawlins leave him to his troubles and head south to another ranch in Coahuila where they find jobs as vaqueros.

Grady falls in love with the beautiful daughter of the Mexican *patrón* of the ranch. The pair become deeply involved, over the objections of her family, notably her aunt. Even as that crisis deepens, a worse turn of fate ensues: Mexican lawmen arrive on the ranch and arrest Grady and Rawlins for their complicity in the Blevins affair. They are taken to a nearby jail, where they rediscover Blevins, who has been in custody for an indeterminate period. Eventually, the boys are taken to a larger and more dangerous jail; on the way, Blevins is summarily executed.

Now imprisoned in a horrific Mexican jail, the two cowboys are forced to fight for survival, and both are badly wounded in knife attacks. Fortunately, they gain their freedom after the family of Grady's erstwhile girlfriend intervenes. After several more incidents and a gunshot wound, Grady returns to Texas, where he discovers his father has died. At this point, he is in possession of the magnificent horse that Blevins once owned, which functions in the story as a symbol both of integrity and of the West itself. In Texas, he faces more legal challenges, but a sympathetic judge eventually absolves him of guilt in any of the incidents and awards him ownership of the stallion.

The story concludes with Grady watching the funeral of one of the Mexican employees who had worked on his grandfather's ranch, a woman who had helped raise him. Intuiting that the last links to his old life are finally broken, he literally rides off into the Texas country on the "pretty horse" who has figured so importantly throughout the novel. It is a classic, cinematic conclusion to an epic western that avoids all the usual clichés of fighting Native Americans, gun battles between ranchers and farmers, cattle rustling, and other tropes of the genre. Instead, *All the Pretty Horses* gives us a gritty, finely wrought picture of the mid-twentieth-century southern border. The crises Grady must deal with are small ones in the face of the vast scale and scope of the West itself, and the horses of the title are the reoccurring leitmotif of honor, courage, and resilience that carries the enduring message of the novel so well.

Chapter Twenty

"The world is quite ruthless in selecting between the dream and the reality, even where we will not."

The novel demands the reader's sustained attention as it proceeds through the young cowboys' small but increasingly dangerous adventures. They lose their innocence and are forced to realize that the world is not a good, safe place; there is a constant sense of danger around the next turn of the trail. The teenagers' ability to face challenge after challenge feels at times like Greek myth set on the western plains: Sisyphus rolling the boulder up the hill, knowing it will come crashing back down again and again. Yet both cowboys, especially Grady, are willing to put their shoulder to the stone and continue the saga. Each undergoes a classic coming-of-age moment in the course of the novel.

Grady as a character appealed to me deeply as I sailed the troubled waters of the Arabian Gulf in those turbulent days of the early 1990s. Just as I finished the novel, I experienced my first combat loss as a leader when a young electrician's mate rushing to do his job under the stress of incoming fire electrocuted himself in the main engineering spaces. As we brought his body up to the main deck and prepared for the helicopter to carry off his remains, I thought strongly of *All the Pretty Horses*.

It was a tragic loss. The young sailor was in his late teens, about the age of John Grady Cole, and should have had a full life ahead of him. Over the long course of my career I lost many, many fine men and women under my command, from the Arabian Gulf to the mountains of Afghanistan to the waters of the western Pacific. I signed hundreds of letters of condolence to grieving families, and each letter represented a deep sense of loss at a life cut short. In the end, the message of *All the Pretty Horses* is about the potential of our youth, the cruel and random events that will challenge us, and the need to keep a sense of perspective as we roll the boulder up the hill. Those are powerful and enduring thoughts.

Over the years, I've dipped back into the novel several times, although I haven't read it cover-to-cover again. Because it is so inextricably tied, for me, to the losses I have suffered over the years, I find it hard to reread, but eventually I will. One point worth knowing is that *All the Pretty Horses* is actually the first (and by far the best) of a trilogy of books, including *The Crossing* and *Cities of the Plain*, which together constitute McCarthy's Border Trilogy. One day, perhaps when I'm headed to Texas for a couple of weeks' visit, I will reread the three books in sequence to understand the full scale of McCarthy's themes. But in the meantime, whenever I learn of a young man or woman whose life thread has been suddenly snipped, I think of *All the Pretty Horses*. The world is a hard place. We will all face our losses, but keeping perspective on them is at the heart of being a leader.

CHAPTER TWENTY-ONE

DEAL IN HOPE

Candide

by Voltaire

> It is love; love, the comfort of the human species, the preserver of the universe, the soul of all sentient beings, love, tender love.

I didn't have to think twice about including this little book on *The Admiral's Bookshelf*. *Candide* is a very short book, but it is full of amusing dialogue, odd twists of fate, a driving and adventurous narrative, and vivid characters. I've read it dozens of times, probably close to annually throughout my adult life. Whenever I am asked to recommend a few of my favorite books, *Candide* is invariably on the list.

Yet, having said that, I am surprised at how few people have actually read it. Admittedly, at first glance it appears to be a frivolous romp with a comical format somewhat reminiscent of *Don*

Quixote. I think that is its greatest strength, but some readers perceive its light tone as a weakness. Some find it silly, sarcastic, or just too cute. But for my money, *Candide* is one of the greatest books about life ever written. Virtually every page offers profound wisdom.

Published in the mid-1700s during the Enlightenment, it is the master work of François-Marie Arouet, a brilliant thinker and marvelous writer better known by his pen name, Voltaire. He lived a long and eventful life, surviving well into his mid-eighties, an extraordinary lifespan for that period. He was an astute and observant participant in many of the turbulent events of the eighteenth century, including the brutal Seven Years' War and the devastating Lisbon earthquake of 1755, both of which influenced Voltaire's views deeply and figure in the novel. The work was commercially successful but considered scandalous when it first appeared. It was often banned in Voltaire's time and afterward, falling in and out of favor over the succeeding centuries, but has settled into the western canon as one of the greatest and most influential books ever written.

Voltaire wrote during a period of intellectual breakthroughs by philosophers and scientists such as John Locke, René Descartes, and Immanuel Kant. The first real stirrings of liberty and antimonarchism flowered during the Enlightenment, and democracy, socialism, and personal liberty blossomed. Of note, the philosophy of optimism, often identified with German polymath Gottfried Wilhelm Leibniz, was a prevalent belief at the time. *Candide* was intended to skewer the naive and unrealistic view that "all is for the best in the best of all possible worlds."

Voltaire knew well that the world was full of tragedy, devastation, disease, political unrest, murder, and rape. Thus, he created in *Candide* a memorable pair of characters to essentially test the theory of the "best possible world." They are Candide himself, a young, handsome idealist; and his mentor and teacher, Professor Pangloss, the philosopher of the court of the Holy Roman Emperor. The professor strongly believes in the ultimate goodness of the world and tries to convince Candide of this view. Candide initially adopts his mentor's views and remains optimistic in the face of adversity as they explore the world. They are accompanied on their journeys by the beautiful Cunegonde, the daughter of a baron.

As this high-speed picaresque novel unfolds, Candide encounters an array of coming-of-age experiences that test his adherence to the philosophy of pure optimism. The novel is arranged into thirty chapters, which themselves are divided by location. The first ten chapters are set in Europe, the second ten are set in the Americas (a place that held deep fascination for Europeans of the Enlightenment), and the final ten take Candide and Pangloss back to Europe, to include a sojourn to the Ottoman Empire.

The novel opens in an opulent castle in eastern Europe where things are going fairly well. Professor Pangloss is tutoring both Candide and Cunegonde. Candide is a privileged but thoroughly likeable young man who is falling in love with Cunegonde. Things quickly go downhill when Candide is evicted from the castle after trying to begin an affair with her. He ends up in the Bulgarian (really the Prussian) military and learns that his new masters have destroyed the castle. Cunegonde, he is told, was brutally raped and then killed.

Candide and Pangloss sally forth to Lisbon, where they see the awful results of the earthquake of 1755 and the following tsunami and fires that nearly destroyed the city. Pangloss, despite all the tragedy they are encountering, continues to espouse a highly optimistic view of the world. Candide and Pangloss are caught up in an auto-da-fé by the Inquisition and are set to be tortured and hanged but manage to survive. To their surprise, they reencounter Cunegonde, who is very much alive, having survived rape and torture herself. Candide rescues her from slavery, and the three of them escape from Lisbon and travel to the Americas, stopping first in Buenos Aires, Argentina.

In the Americas, more travails unfold, and Candide has to flee to Paraguay to stay ahead of the Inquisition. Somewhere along this portion of the voyage Candide acquires a servant, Cacambo, and together they encounter a variety of native Americans in South America. They discover El Dorado, the legendary city where the streets were said to be paved with gold and jewels. They journey on north to Suriname on the Caribbean coast of South America, where they meet Martin, a decidedly pessimistic philosopher who joins the entourage. Nearly continuous arguments over philosophy result, with Candide remaining (unrealistically) optimistic about the state of the world, still very much a student of Pangloss. I think most readers are siding with the pessimistic Martin at this point, given the events of the trip.

Finally, they return to Europe via Bordeaux and Paris, arriving in England just in time to see an admiral shot for failing to succeed in battle against the French fleet. This episode is based on an actual event in which the British crown executed Admiral John Byng for failing to press the enemy hard enough in battle. The execution is explained to Candide in one of the most famous lines in the novel, as he is told that every so often the British find it necessary to kill an admiral in order to "encourage the others." I've used that line (in jest) from time to time, mostly in after-dinner toasts.

Candide moves on to Venice, where he learns that Cunegonde is now in Istanbul. He heads off to that city and discovers that the once-beautiful Cunegonde, beaten down by life, has lost her looks and is working as a dishwasher for a Balkan prince.

Candide rescues Cunegonde, who is more than happy to depart the Ottoman Empire. On a positive note, Candide manages to discover Professor Pangloss as well and frees him from horrific captivity as a rower in a slave galley. In a seemingly happy ending, Candide, Cunegonde, Pangloss, Cacambo, and several other characters obtain their freedom and end up together on a tiny farm back in Europe.

In their penultimate journey they seek wisdom from a wise dervish. When Candide asks the question at the heart of his searching—why do humans suffer so much?—the dervish says, in essence, that God cares not a whit about men. They are no more than mice on a ship sailing to a destination they cannot even comprehend. The dervish abruptly concludes the conversation by simply slamming the door on the group, leaving them to articulate their own philosophy of life.

Candide, Pangloss, and the others set off to return to the farm. Along the way they encounter one final character, a Turk who tells them that he is a farmer also, and that he works hard in order to avoid the great evils of boredom, vice, and poverty. The entire cast—Candide, Pangloss, Cunegonde, Cacambo, and others—are reunited at the end of the book on their own farm, and decide as the book ends: "Let us tend our garden."

"Let us tend our garden."

What to make of this short but vibrant story?

First and most obviously it tells us that a Pollyanna style of blind optimism is foolish. A philosophy of pure optimism ignores the brutal realities of life, all of which Candide and his fellow travelers experience. Readers have the luxury of learning this fundamental truth without undergoing all the misadventures of the cast of *Candide*, fortunately. But it is a crucial lesson of the book: many things are likely *not going to turn out well*. The sooner we recognize that simple fact, the better.

A second, and equally powerful, lesson is that when faced with life's challenges, there is a path to whatever happiness we can attain in this flawed world if we figuratively "tend our gardens." This means that despite life's "slings and arrows," we must avoid the pitfall of depression and other failures like succumbing to boredom, vice, and poverty. Like Sisyphus, we must continue to put our shoulder to the stone, even knowing that inevitably it will roll back down again.

> "Our labor preserves us from three great evils—boredom, vice, and poverty."

Third, *Candide* shows us that humor can help us in the darkest times. No matter how viciously life lashes out against Candide and the other hapless protagonists, they manage to survive by largely avoiding self-pity and seeing the irony in their circumstances. Obviously, this is easier to recommend (and write into a fictional novel) than it is to do in real life. But the novel provides a good blueprint for the ways humor (and perspective) can sustain us in difficult times.

Another major theme is simply love. There is much love in the novel between all the characters, despite their occasional bickering and complaining. And Candide, simple, naive Candide, comes again and again to the rescue of his fellow travelers. Voltaire seems to be telling us that when we are faced by adversity, love can help us sail through toward an end—like Candide—surrounded by friends and family as we tend the metaphorical garden of our lives.

Finally, *Candide* is a brilliant example of parody. By pointing out the absurdity and seeming randomness of life, Voltaire is saying to each of us, look, don't take this too seriously. Pompous people (like Professor Pangloss) are everywhere, and they are usually wrong. Just as we turn on *Saturday Night Live* every week to see the powerful mocked, we likewise can turn the clock back almost three hundred years and find the same remedy in the form of this novel. *Candide* mocks corrupt governments, vicious dictators, British courts-martial, evil slaveholders, murders and rapists, and the Roman Catholic church in bold and convincing terms. That strain of politically useful satire continues to this day on late-night talk shows and editorial cartoons—with powerful effect.

Candide epitomizes the very heart of my life philosophy. I have always believed in Napoleon's dictum that "a leader is a dealer in hope." This does *not* mean, by the way, that leaders should ever minimize challenges or simply assume that everything will turn out well in the end. As the wise saying goes, "hope is not a strategy." But what *is* a very effective strategy, in my long experience of leadership, is believing in the ultimate goodness of people and approaching them with a positive, upbeat vision of where you want to take your command. A leader, like Candide himself, needs to be that dealer in hope—not in fear, or in chaos, but rather a realistically positive view of the world.

I've discovered that people will almost always turn out to be what you expect them to be. If you are suspicious and skeptical of your team and constantly tell them how dire the situation ahead is likely to be, you will find your team shaken and unmotivated. If, on the other hand, you tell them, and demonstrate, that you believe in them and encourage them to excel, they most often will do exactly that. I've found this to be true from my first days as a division officer with a couple of dozen Sailors under me on a destroyer in the western Pacific to leading NATO with 3 million men and women under arms, most of them volunteers. Optimism matters in leadership at every level.

In chapter 3 of this book, "Be Your Own Spokesman," I wrote that of all the leaders I have seen, the best in this regard was Gen. Colin Powell. He had a clear-eyed view of the world, most certainly, but he believed in his people and conveyed that sense of (cautious) optimism to everyone. He was not a "cheerleader," a quality I dislike in a leader, but rather a smart, savvy, and humorous captain at the helm of the ship. You could drop a plumb line from the eighteenth-century story of Candide to the soldier's philosophy of Colin Powell. It is one I've tried to practice along my own voyage.

A final thought: I remember first reading Voltaire at Annapolis as a very young midshipman and laughing at Candide's trials and tribulations. It seemed a funny, lighthearted book about very dark events. But when I got to the fleet and had real Sailors working for me in tough situations in the South China Sea and the Arabian Gulf, the book took on a very different tone. It was still a romp through life, but I began to see the real point Voltaire sought to make for the reader: life is going to be a hard slog for everyone, but if you approach it with a sensible level of optimism, see the reality but not the impossibility of winning the fight that is ahead, and keep your shoulder to the stone like Sisyphus, well, that is as good a prescription as you can have for life.

Voltaire also said that in the end, life is shipwreck and we should all save what we can. Another good toast, and a tribute to a fine writer; but most important, a lesson for the ages. Deal in hope and tend your garden, recognizing there will be real challenges in your voyage; facing them with equanimity is what makes a life worth living.

CHAPTER TWENTY-TWO

KNOW YOUR PROFESSION

The United States Navy
by Capt. Edward L. Beach, USN (Ret.)

> Our navy has its own ideals, prejudices, traditions and deep-set problems. Unexpected changes in technology, politics, or diplomacy will affect it. We all have the right to try to influence the outcome.

No matter what career you choose to pursue, it is critical that you learn not only how to function in that world but also about those who went before you, how the occupation has grown and changed, and where you fit along the arc of its history. I'll illustrate in this chapter that progression for me. That course was set when I first met Capt. Ned Beach in Annapolis at the old headquarters of the U.S. Naval Institute (the professional organization of the nation's sea services) in the mid-1980s. He had been retired for about two decades at that point, but his passion for the profession of being an officer in the U.S. Navy was still very evident. I was a young lieutenant commander forty years his junior, and the depth and breadth of his naval career was simply unimaginable to me.

During a small luncheon at the headquarters organized by the head of the institute, I had a chance to ask him what had made him the proudest in the course of the more than thirty years he spent on active duty. He pushed back from the table a bit and looked out the window over the wintery Naval Academy yard with a distant look in his eyes as if searching for a far horizon. Rather than answering my question, he said that at the very end of World War II he had wondered how it was that he had been spared while so many of his submariner contemporaries had died in their boats. I'll never forget what he said next: "What divided us, the living from the dead? Why me?"

But then he went on to say that what made him happiest and proudest in his career was not all the accolades and honors, the medals and the presidential citations. What made him happiest, he said to me, was to be part of a profession he shared with his father. He told me that being part of the profession of being a naval officer was what counted most for him. In the preface to his extraordinary history of the U.S. Navy, he says, "Both my father and I loved the navy, wrote books and articles about it, served on the board of the U.S. Naval Institute, and read naval history as a special area of personal interest." He goes on, "To my mind and heart, Father never left the navy, nor have I, though his days at sea were over when I knew him, and so, now, are mine (pp. xxi–xxii).

His comments have always stuck with me. At that point in my career, I was still thinking about possibly resigning my commission and perhaps taking a Ph.D. in international affairs and becoming a professor. Later in my career I also toyed with the idea of going back to graduate school yet again and pursuing a law degree, something I'd put on hold years earlier when the Navy sent me to Tufts University and I earned my doctorate at the Fletcher School of Law and Diplomacy. But I came away from the conversation with Captain Beach thinking that as a naval officer I was part of a true and proud *profession*. From that point forward, and continuing to this day nearly forty years later, I've seen myself as a professional naval officer.

A look at the life and times of Ned Beach is a good way to understand what that means. Born in New York in 1918, he graduated at the top of his class at Annapolis in 1939. He trained in diesel submarines and sailed on a series of them in World War II. Of note, in USS *Trigger* in 1943 he was part of the mission that attacked and nearly destroyed a brand-new Japanese carrier—in Tokyo Harbor. He went on to serve in another diesel, USS *Tirante*, sinking at least nine Japanese vessels and receiving the nation's second-highest decoration for combat, the Navy Cross.

After the war, Beach commanded several other submarines, notably USS *Triton*, one of the earliest and largest nuclear-powered subs. Under his command in 1960, *Triton* became the first sub to voyage around the world submerged, departing Groton, Connecticut, in February and sailing underwater for more than 30,000 miles in 61 days. He received the Legion of Merit from the hand of President Eisenhower for the feat. He was widely regarded as one of the best pure seamen ever to command warships, in both combat and peacetime.

But in addition to a sterling professional reputation earned at sea, Beach was a passionate student of his profession. He read prodigiously and built a highly regarded personal library, but above all, he wrote. Over the course of his life he published a dozen books and hundreds of articles on a wide range of professional naval subjects. Of note, his first best-selling novel, *Run Silent, Run Deep* (1955), is still studied in war colleges and at the

Naval Academy for its telling portrayal of the moral challenges posed by tension between the boat's captain and the second in command. It became a popular and well-regarded film in 1958, with Burt Lancaster and Clark Gable starring.

I own many of Beach's books, including the three novels *Run Silent, Run Deep*; *Dust on the Sea*; and *Cold Is the Sea*. All three are vibrant portraits of life in submarines during war and peace and are still popular with submariners. Beach also produced two powerful memoirs. *From Annapolis to Scapa Flow: The Autobiography of Edward L. Beach, Sr.* is a lovingly edited biography of his father; *Salt and Steel: Reflections of a Submariner* is his own story.

Finally, he also directly contributed to the profession he loved by writing seven highly regarded professional works of nonfiction. Of those, the best three are *Around the World Submerged: The Voyage of the* Triton; *The Wreck of the* Memphis; and, of course, *The United States Navy: 200 Years*. I have read the latter several times, and I have always found it a superb work of professional writing. It manages to fuse powerful writing from the pen of a master with the immense professional background Captain Beach brought to the task of telling the Navy's story.

At the lunch I had with him, I naturally asked what new book he was working on. His face lit up, and he said he was writing the biography of the U.S. Navy. He was at pains to say that he was not himself a naval historian, although he loved and read deeply in the genre. "But what I am," I can remember him saying, "is a Sailor with a lot of actual experience." In the author's note of that book, he says, "There are essentially two views of history: that which one has studied, and that which one has experienced. It is not possible to combine the two." Fortunately for our profession, Ned Beach chose to tell the story as he learned it, adding the power of his deep personal experience to produce a first-rate book.

And that brings us to the most powerful point to take away from *The United States Navy: 200 Years*. The Navy has been fueled and driven by professionals—naval officers, chief petty officers, petty officers, and Sailors who share a handful of traits that make them part of this historic profession.

First, and the obvious reason I selected it for this volume, is that the naval profession has a documented, respected, and continuing body of literature that recounts its history. Seagoing professionals know that studying the history of their profession is part of their responsibility to the art and craft of being a Sailor. This is equally true for other professions, of course, from engineers to physicians to attorneys to educators. Each profession has a history its practitioners must inculcate and study. It is hard to imagine a single volume that more personifies that requirement than Captain Beach's history of the Navy.

A second aspect of a profession is the documentation of *how* to perform the tasks that are required to practice it. Countless books have been written—and are constantly updated—dealing with the conduct of maritime operations, tactics at sea, and the conduct of combat on the world's oceans. Over the years, I have contributed to that part of the profession with the publication of books about ship handling and watch standing (*Watch Officer's Guide*); leadership on the deck plates (*Division Officer's Guide*); and the most essential task of a naval professional, serving as the captain of a warship (*Command at Sea*). Certainly, meeting Captain Beach and reading his books inspired me in those efforts.

The third part of being a professional is participating in its professional organization(s). In the case of the nation's sea services (Navy, Coast Guard, Merchant Marine, Marine Corps), that organization is the U.S. Naval Institute. I have been a proud member for decades and frequently publish in its monthly journal, *Proceedings*. Like Captain Beach, I've served on the board, contributed to it financially, and published professional books, including the one you are reading now. I have tried to pass my enthusiasm along to more junior members of the profession. This is, of course, equally true in other professions and organizations; the American Medical Association and the American Bar Association are civilian examples.

Fourth, and finally, a profession is marked by participation in ongoing education and improvement. This can be done by self-study using the type of books and professional journals just discussed. Another vital part of this is participating in conferences, lectures, symposia, and other gatherings of the profession. The Naval Institute hosts one of the largest such events each year in San Diego (often in partnership with other professional organizations such as the Armed Forces Communications and Electronics Association). There are likewise dozens of smaller gatherings in the Pentagon and in fleet concentration areas such as Norfolk, Virginia; Mayport, Florida; and Pearl Harbor, Hawaii, to name a few.

The reason this book makes *The Admiral's Bookshelf* is quite simple: it epitomizes the idea of studying and immersing yourself in your chosen profession. By picking it up and reading it—easily done, as it is quite conversational in tone—you learn the very roots of the U.S. Navy, back to the earliest days of the Revolutionary War. Understanding the way the young Navy comported itself in that conflict and then morphed into a force that fought Barbary pirates and then England once again in the early 1800s is mandatory for today's Sailor seeking to understand who we are as a fighting force.

I think an essential part of a leader's job is to become immersed in the specific details of the chosen profession. Only with that deep knowledge can a leader do what is necessary not only to ensure that the profession itself prospers, but also that its junior members are developing as they should. When I was the Supreme Allied Commander of NATO, I held monthly book talks. We would invite an important author to visit the NATO operational headquarters in Mons, Belgium, and speak about a recently released book. Gary Shteyngart's presentation of his brilliant satire about post-Soviet Russia, *Absurdistan*, comes to mind. We invited historian Roger Crowley to talk about the pivotal battle of Lepanto as depicted in his history, *Empires of the Sea*. We also showed important films about the military profession and encouraged junior officers to publish their thoughts in professional journals. Keeping books like *The United States Navy: 200 Years* at the forefront for professionals is a key part of leadership.

Captain Beach also analyzes the shifting technology that has accompanied the Navy's development, from the opening chapter, where he talks about the role of specific types of trees used for ship construction, through the age of sail and rifled guns, the transition into coal and oil, the advent of radar and sonar, and eventually to his own beloved nuclear power. The way he weaves together the threads of combat with the advances of technology is in essence the story of the naval profession.

The narrative builds to the crescendo of World War II, "Armageddon at Sea." In opening the final part of the book that deals with the war, he says, "If it can be said that our navy had only [limited hours] of combat experience prior to World War II, it can also be said that World War II was one long gigantic battle with almost unrelieved stress on all participants. Respite[s] in harbor were conspicuously few." He describes the Battle of Midway in spare, crisp prose and puts the profound significance of that victory in terms that have helped make annual "Battle of Midway" dinners mandatory attendance events for U.S. naval professionals around the world. The battle remains one of the most pivotal in history, akin to Salamis in ancient Greece, Lepanto in the Middle Ages, and Trafalgar in the Napoleonic era.

The book closes with an epilogue and a few thoughts on the postwar navy. Reflecting the world situation in 1986, when it was written, this small chapter is a perfect example of why the idea of a profession matters. It provides a thoughtful analysis about how the Navy should be shaped for the continuing, draining Cold War with the Soviet Union. Drawing on the profound wisdom of Rear Adm. Alfred Thayer Mahan, Captain Beach concludes this seminal book by sketching a realistic strategy for the United States upon the oceans of the world.

A few years ago, as Laura and I entered our sixties, we decided it was time to find a place for us to be buried together when our time comes. Having spent so much of our lives in the Navy (both Laura and I grew up in naval families, as Ned Beach did), we thought the Naval Academy cemetery would be a good choice. It is a very small piece of land—a few acres only—on Hospital Point in Annapolis, abutting the Severn River and the Chesapeake Bay.

As we worked with the office of the superintendent to find just the right spot, I discovered the burial plot of Captain Ned Beach at the edge of the cemetery. He sleeps in the shadow of Beach Hall, the headquarters of the U.S. Naval Institute, which helped shape both our lives and is appropriately named for him. Laura and I decided then to request that our plots be nearby, with a good view out over the river and the trees, and behind us the solid walls of Beach Hall. I'm proud to know that one day my wife and I will sail in company with Capt. Ned Beach, a fellow sea captain, a gifted and creative writer, and a professional at the foremost ranks of the U.S. Navy. His marvelous book, *The U.S. Navy: 200 Years*, is most deserving of its place on *The Admiral's Bookshelf*.

Godspeed and open water, Cap'n Beach. One day I'll join up alongside—hopefully not too soon!

CHAPTER TWENTY-THREE

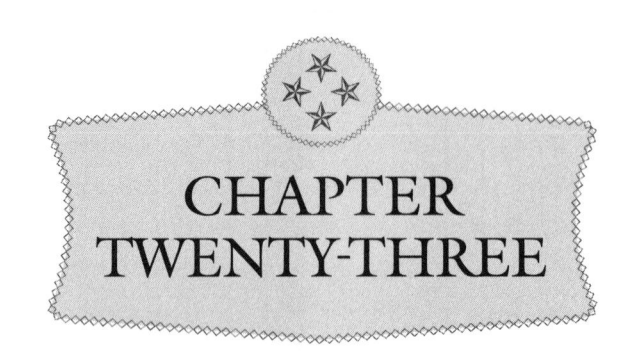

SEE THE DANGER

Nineteen Eighty-Four
by George Orwell

> The best books . . . are those that tell you
> what you know already.

It is human nature to try to look into the future and predict what might be around the next bend in the road. We do this in our personal lives, of course, wondering how our individual stories will turn out: our relationships, careers, friendships, investments—the small wins and losses of our individual voyages. Many of us also think about where the world is headed, because such knowledge can help us frame important individual decisions ranging from where to invest our money, to which career we choose, to the advice we offer our friends and families. I've certainly done so throughout my life.

Naturally, as we think about where the world is headed, we should be getting our data and predictions from accurate, factual sources. That might be *Economist* magazine, *Foreign Affairs* magazine published by the Council on Foreign Relations, the *Harvard Business School Review*, or even the various scholarly books that make predictions about the future. An example of the latter might be Graham Allison's *Destined for War: Can America and China Avoid the Thucydides Trap*, or Elbridge Colby's *Strategy of Denial* about defending Taiwan. Likewise, looking in the rearview mirror at history and biography can help us understand the past and allow us to think about how we can apply what has already happened to the future. Both are very helpful techniques.

But for me, an additional powerful resource in that process may surprise you: novels. I've always tried to incorporate into my crystal ball the best books of imaginative fiction that hypothesize what might come next in the form of surprising plot twists. Some books along those lines are very hopeful, positing a world with challenges and turmoil but with goodness triumphing: an example would be *The Lord of the Rings* (which some critics think is loosely based on the events of World War II). But some of the best books of prognostication are dark indeed and serve us best by helping us think about what might happen if things *don't* turn out well.

The most frightening book I've ever read in that vein has the simplest title: *Nineteen Eighty-Four*. It was written in 1949, just after the end of World War II, and set in what at the time was the somewhat distant future toward the end of the twentieth century. The book is about a society under totalitarian control and was intended by its author to serve as a warning to the world about the dangers of dictators, thought control, and repression—all threats that were becoming clear at the time, especially in the Soviet Union and previously in Nazi Germany.

George Orwell was a pen name of the socially active political writer and essayist Eric Arthur Blair. Orwell is also well known for the novella *Animal Farm*, an allegorical work that shines a highly critical light on communism and Stalin's Russia. While the story takes place in a barnyard with talking animals, this is no children's book. *Nineteen Eighty-Four*, which appeared four years after *Animal Farm*, takes an even darker approach, leading the reader to consider the very worst aspects of political control. Between them, the two books have brought terms such as "Big Brother," "newspeak," "doublethink," and "thought police" into the modern lexicon. The books are a massive blinking caution light essentially begging Western democratic societies to avoid falling victim to the horrors of dictatorships, fascism, communism, and thought control.

Nineteen Eighty-Four, set in a fictional version of Great Britain in the year of the title, foresees a world of virtually endless war. Airstrip One, the small province where the action is set, has been subjugated by the much larger nation of Oceania, which includes much of North and South America and Australia. Two other major states exist in this dystopian world, both of which are totalitarian entities: Eurasia dominates Russia and western Europe, and Eastasia is centered on China. The leader of Oceania is Big Brother, a ruthless dictator propped up by an immense personality cult generated by a KGB-like entity known as the "thought police." That term, of course, is used widely in twenty-first-century America and the West, although in an entirely different context.

Oceania and its global competitors are dominated by overarching and pervasive government surveillance, constant propaganda, and manipulation of every aspect of "truth." The story opens with the introduction of a protagonist who is a tiny cog in the huge wheel of government, Winston Smith. His role is to be part of what the Party does every day: exert control over society.

> "Everything faded into mist. The past was erased, the erasure was forgotten, the lie became truth."

Winston Smith is an agent of that process of erasure.

As a Party member, Winston's specific job at the enormous Ministry of Truth is to rewrite history so that it conforms to whatever the government currently believes it should be. Truthful documents deemed contrary to policy are literally dropped into "memory holes" and sent to a constantly burning underground furnace. Winston secretly despises his society but is fearful of being exposed as a criminal, so he carries on with his job. He is an unwilling participant in the overall effort that proclaims three key slogans: "War is peace," indicating unity in hatred; "Freedom is slavery," urging individuals to find themselves only in the Party; and "Ignorance is strength," which means that the Party knows best.

In the proletarian quarter, where less privileged citizens live, he obtains a diary and begins to write down opposing thoughts. Soon he encounters Julia, a like-minded worker in the Ministry whose job is to meld fiction to the norms of the government. Smith also meets several mysterious characters who may (or may not) be part of an underground resistance movement. He eventually begins an affair with Julia, although he has doubts about the sincerity of her commitment to overthrowing the regime.

Against the backdrop of their affair, we learn of a shadowy revolutionary organization, the Brotherhood. Even as those relationships unfold, geopolitics shifts Oceania's enemy from Eurasia to Eastasia, necessitating much more work at the Ministry to reshape the truth into compliance with the new geopolitical reality (this mirrors the shift of Russia from an enemy aligned with Hitler to a friend and ally during World War II). Winston is increasingly drawn into the complex web of domestic politics.

Tragedy strikes suddenly when an undercover agent based in the proletarian quarter betrays Winston and Julia. They are captured, imprisoned, starved, and brutally tortured. As the tension in this portion of the book reaches a crescendo, Winston is taken to the infamous Room 101, in which captives are forced to confront their worst fears—in his case rats. His resistance collapses, and he betrays his lover.

> "If you want to keep a secret, you must also hide it from yourself."

Broken in body and spirit, he pledges fealty to the Party and is released back into society. He personally experienced the frightening process at the heart of the Party, that "power is in tearing human minds to pieces and putting them together again in new shapes of your own choosing." By the end of *Nineteen Eighty-Four*, the shattered minds of Winston and Julia have been reassembled to prevent any future threat to the dominance of the Party or Big Brother.

In a sad and heart-wrenching denouement, Winston encounters Julia, who, he realizes, must have similarly betrayed him. "Two gin-scented tears trickled down the sides of his nose." But Winston thinks, "But it was all right, everything was all right, the struggle was finished. He had won the victory over himself." What the reader correctly sees is the opposite, of course: the state, the Party, and Big Brother were the only winners.

Nineteen Eighty-Four was an instant classic, selling tens of thousands of copies in Great Britain and the United States on its release. It has since sold more than 30 million copies, has been translated into more than 60 languages, and is routinely on the lists of the top English-language novels ever published. Even the use of the year as a title (something Orwell and his publisher disagreed about, with Orwell prevailing) has become a standard literary device.

Indeed, when I set out several years ago, almost eighty years after Orwell, to write a cautionary story about geopolitics in the twenty-first century, my coauthor and I selected the title *2034: A Novel of the Next World War* in homage to George Orwell's brilliance in creating a future world that any sane reader would reject. The sequel to that book, *2054: A Novel*, adds the dangers of artificial intelligence and civil conflict in America to the geopolitical mix in that year. It appeared early in 2024. The final book in our trilogy will conclude a century after Orwell's tale with a very different cautionary story: *2084: A Novel of War and Climate*. Focusing a reader's mind on a specific year when doling out a dose of caution is a powerful device.

So, what are we to make of *Nineteen Eighty-Four* in our twenty-first-century world? Why did I include it in *The Admiral's Bookshelf*?

First, it is a powerful example of the highest and best use of literature—its highest-order purpose. The book uses powerful, driven prose to tell a compelling and tragic story full of memorable scenes and phrases. Good literature can serve many purposes, of course. It can amuse us and gentle the soul or fill us with wonder at the beauty of the world. A good book can also transport us to a more fascinating world. American writer Jack Kerouac accomplishes this in *On the Road*, a bawdy romp through midcentury America. Similarly, a fine novel can challenge us to think what we would do if faced with a difficult decision, such as the one Atticus Finch makes in *To Kill a Mockingbird*. We can use literature as a kind of simulator that places us in a challenging situation and see if we would have the courage and fortitude to make the right decision under extreme pressure.

Cautionary fiction demands that we look at something terrible and wonder "could that really happen here?" And if the answer is yes, the same book demands that we respond with action to avoid such a perilous outcome. We must approach that task knowing, as Orwell tells us in *Nineteen Eighty-Four*, that "the further a society drifts from the truth, the more it will hate those that speak it." The ability and willingness to think through worst-case scenarios is particularly critical for leaders. They must be able to inspire their subordinates to take such potentially frightening scenarios seriously and construct the plans necessary to push back against them. These are tasks that fall within the remit of any serious leader. I remember when I was NATO commander initially failing to see the serious threat Vladimir Putin posed to the Western alliance. Fortunately, the leaders of the Baltic states convinced me of his intentions. They did the right thing by almost literally grabbing me by the lapels in 2013 and saying, "He will invade again, and much closer to NATO." A year later, he marched into Ukraine for the first time. Leaders, above all, must see the danger.

We certainly see Orwellian (a word thoroughly grounded in the zeitgeist of today) aspects of life in a variety of totalitarian countries around the world. The mullahs of Tehran seek to enforce their puritanical vision of Shi'a Islam on a vast population. They have torture chambers, personality cults, "revolutionary guards," and powerful intelligence services at their disposal. Yet we see occasional flickers of resistance rise in Iran, most recently in nationwide protests after the death of an innocent young woman in the hands of the ironically named "morality police." As the war in Ukraine grinds on, we see in Russia the imposition of government-vetted and literally created "truth" in terms of casualty rates, economic challenges, and brutal crackdowns on courageous journalists. While Putin's Russia is not (yet) Oceania, it is edging closer to it.

Here in the West, and particularly in the United States, we see echoes of this kind of propaganda, thought control, and enforced orthodoxy of thought in a place we should never have expected it: our university system. Increasingly, polls show that students are afraid to be fully honest about their views because they fear offending their classmates or professors. This is especially true for conservative students in the largely liberal domain of higher education, but there are examples across the political spectrum. Recent confrontations on college campuses between Jewish students and those who support Palestinian causes have increased tensions. Above all, our universities should be places where differences of thought and belief are fully tolerated, and indeed encouraged. Yet students and faculty worry about what they literally refer to as the campus "thought police."

What concerns me most when I look ahead is the danger presented by artificial intelligence and the possibilities it offers to governments seeking to control the populace. With its almost unlimited ability to create deep fake videos, doctored speeches, robotic and ghost texts, and false phone calls that sound like political figures reaching out to individual voters, AI has the potential to do massive damage to democratic nations. A healthy democracy is at the heart of a valid electoral process. When that is threatened by new technologies coupled with old-fashioned demagogues and political operatives, we have moved a step or two closer to Oceania.

Which is why all of us, as we read powerful novels like *Nineteen Eighty-Four*, must translate them into the present and push back against the forces that would move us thus. We should be supporting efforts to identify media products produced by AI, effectively putting a "this could be false" trademark stamp on such messages and videos. Likewise, we must be alert to the strong possibility that AI might be used to create new "realities." The most Orwellian of the terms that have emerged in the past few years is "fake news," a term used by many miscreants to gloss over or simply disregard their wrongdoing. Yet, ironically, there is a grain of truth in their protests; there *is* in fact more and more fake news, often generated on a large scale by political organizations. Additionally, we need to cherish free speech and a wide range of political views in our democracy, and especially on college campuses.

Sadly, I see no easy answers here. At this stage, the most important thing we can and must do is also the simplest: *see the danger*. Then we need to do all we can—in our own personal, electoral, and policy choices—to avoid allowing free societies to drift down the dangerous path charted by George Orwell nearly a century ago. The Internet, soon to be powered by AI, can continue to be a powerful tool for good. But the possibility that political demagogues will use it to lead their nations down the path of *Nineteen Eighty-Four* is growing greater. See the danger. It is right there, hovering just in front of us. Be ready.

CHAPTER TWENTY-FOUR

REACH FOR GLORY CAREFULLY
The Great Gatsby
by F. Scott Fitzgerald

> He knew that when he kissed this girl, and forever wed his unutterable visions to her perishable breath, his mind would never romp again like the mind of God. So he waited, listening for a moment longer to the tuning fork that had been struck upon a star. Then he kissed her.

I vacillated about including this novel in *The Admiral's Bookshelf*. It was published a century ago, in 1925, and has certainly withstood the test of time with critics. *The Great Gatsby* is still in print and appears on virtually every list of the great novels ever published in English. It remains a mainstay in high school and college literature programs.

Yet I hesitated because of the paradox at the heart of the novel: is Jay Gatsby, née Gatz, the self-invented creation of an ambitious young man, a *good* example of what we think of as the American dream? Did he legitimately make himself in the ways—imagination, audacity, risk-taking, hard work—that we believe are the right ways to achieve our goals? Or was his entire persona one big lie, and his success achieved in illegitimate and indeed illegal ways? In short, is Gatsby himself a good example or a cautionary story?

> "So he invented just the sort of Jay Gatsby that a seventeen year old boy would be likely to invent, and to this conception he was faithful to the end."

Let's start with the author, F. Scott Fitzgerald. He led a golden life in his early years, born to an upper-middle-class family in Minnesota and sent to Ivy League Princeton for college. Handsome and athletic, he seemed on the path to literary success and financial security until he fell in love with a fellow student at Princeton, Ginevra King. When her upper-class family rejected Fitzgerald's suit, he enlisted in the U.S. Army in the lead-up to World War I and obtained a commission in the infantry.

The Army posted him to the Deep South, where he met and fell in love with Zelda Sayre, a beautiful but emotionally unstable southern belle. Still smarting from Ginevra's rejection, he rushed into marriage with Zelda. His writing career took off after the war with the publication of two best-selling novels chronicling the story of his generation: *This Side of Paradise* (1920) and *The Beautiful and the Damned* (1922), both of which are still well regarded. *Gatsby*, on the other hand, was released in 1925 to mostly middling reviews and was initially a sales disappointment, although it subsequently sold more than 30 million copies and has been translated into more than 40 languages.

Set in trendy Long Island in the very early 1920s, before the Great Depression, *The Great Gatsby* is a short novel with strong literary drive. It is narrated by Nick Carraway, a bonds salesman and World War I veteran. Nick rents a tiny bungalow in the fictitious village of West Egg on a small plot of land next door to an enormous mansion—the residence of the mysterious millionaire Jay Gatsby. Nick can hear the raucous parties held there night after night but seems indifferent to not being invited. In many ways, Nick is the moral center of the book, a man striving to improve his place in the world but not initially caught up in the whirling immorality and bountiful wealth of the Roaring Twenties.

Things change when Nick reconnects with his wealthy cousin, Daisy Buchanan. She is a friend from his youth, now married to a Yale man and football star, the enormously wealthy Tom Buchanan. Daisy and Tom have moved to the more fashionable East Egg and live in a mansion literally across the sound from Gatsby's huge home; their dock features a beckoning green light. Nick disapproves of Tom when he learns that Tom has a slutty mistress, Myrtle Wilson, who lives in a trashy part of town (referred to symbolically as the valley of ashes) between Long Island and New York City. Nick is gradually drawn into the Buchanans' orbit and starts to date an acquaintance of theirs, a nationally ranked amateur golfer named Jordan Baker (whom he later learns is suspected of cheating in matches).

Eventually, Nick is invited to one of the parties at Gatsby's home. When he attends, more out of curiosity than real desire, he finally meets the title character. He likes Gatsby, although he finds several aspects of his personality odd, particularly his stories about his service in the European theater during the war. And yet, Nick says, "He had one of those rare smiles with a quality of eternal reassurance in it, that you may come across four or five times in life." Gatsby tries to develop a deeper relationship with Nick, who learns that Gatsby is hopelessly in love with Daisy. He met her (as Fitzgerald met Zelda) in the South while he was awaiting deployment into combat. When Gatsby left, Daisy rushed into marriage with Tom. Using Nick and his cottage as a base, Gatsby begins an affair with Daisy.

Tom Buchanan discovers the affair and is furious (ignoring the fact that he has had multiple affairs and is currently carrying on with Myrtle). A climactic confrontation takes place between Gatsby and Tom at an apartment where the lovers have been meeting. Afterward, Daisy and Gatsby leave in Gatsby's car, with Daisy driving. The car strikes and kills Myrtle. Myrtle's distraught husband, George, seeks revenge against Gatsby, whom he is led by Tom to believe was driving the car. George goes to Gatsby's mansion and shoots and kills Gatsby, then turns the gun on himself.

When Gatsby's father arrives to attend his son's funeral, one of the few mourners, Nick realizes how vapid and meaningless the Buchanans' lives really were. He now understands that his future lies not in glitzy and corrupt New York, but back in his native Midwest. Thus ends the story of Jay Gatsby.

It is worth knowing that the novel is a bit of a roman à clef; that is, the characters are largely based on real individuals whom the Fitzgeralds knew. This gives the action a sense of reality even amid the book's highly symbolic plot and characters. The key themes of the novel are timeless and appropriate for America, and one of my professors at Annapolis called it the true "great American novel." Indeed, Fitzgerald's preferred title for it was *Under the Red, White, and Blue.*

The American dream tropes are all present in the novel. They include pulling yourself up by your bootstraps and accomplishing whatever you want by dint of hard work, a preference for self-made wealth over inherited (and therefore inherently corrupt) money, and cynicism toward the privileges of the super-rich. The love triangle between wealthy, corrupt, racist, white supremacist Tom Buchanan; self-made, hardworking, daring Jay Gatsby; and the vapid but desirable southern belle Daisy Buchanan illustrates those themes brilliantly. In the end, we find that both Tom Buchanan and Jay Gatsby are flawed characters, Tom with his philandering and heartless arrogance, and Jay with his shady business practices and false representations about his background.

It would have been easy for Fitzgerald to make Gatsby an entirely likeable war hero who made his money strictly legally and had high moral standards. He then would have stood diametrically opposed to the darkly corrupt Tom Buchanan. Instead, Fitzgerald gives us a shaded portrait of a man who is fundamentally good but, given the inherent challenges in an unjust and unequal world, has to allow himself some leeway in both his business practices and his representations about himself. This moral complexity is what makes the novel so extraordinary and compelling in America, where few actors on our national scene are perfect, to say the least.

The novel is also a highly symbolic work of literature, with each character having a specific role. Some of the best writing is found in the characterizations of the relatively minor characters, from the cool, languid golf cheat Jordan Baker to the over-the-top trashiness of Myrtle Wilson. Even the real Jewish gangster Arnold Rothstein (who famously fixed the 1919 World Series) makes a brief but important appearance as Meyer Wolfsheim in a shadowy scene meant to show the reader that Gatsby's money has a dark foundation.

Another highly symbolic moment occurs when Gatsby is showing Daisy his wardrobe and begins throwing hundreds of beautiful shirts in dozens of colors into the air. Daisy is enraptured by their beauty as they float to the ground, but for the reader they represent the mindless wealth Gatsby has accumulated. "Suddenly with a strained sound Daisy bent her head into the shirts and began to cry stormily. 'They're such beautiful shirts,' she sobbed, her voice muffled in the thick folds. 'It makes me sad because I've never seen such—such beautiful shirts before.'" That scene is highlighted in both of the two superb films based on the book, one starring Robert Redford in the title role (1974) and the other, more recent one with Leonardo DiCaprio as Gatsby (2013).

When I first read *The Great Gatsby*, I was a high school junior preparing to head off to Annapolis. The fundamental theme that leaped out at me then, and still does today, is the flamboyance of Gatsby's vision of himself. Jay Gatz dared to envision himself marrying well above his social class when he fell in love with Daisy (much as Fitzgerald did in loving Ginevra King). "So he invented just the sort of Jay Gatsby that a seventeen-year-old boy would be likely to invent, and to this conception he was faithful to the end." To do that, he needed to reinvent himself and achieve the kind of wealth that would allow him to compete for her hand. He steadily set out to do so, using all the skills and tools he could muster, to include blind ambition, deep audacity, a willingness to bend the legal process in business, and above all to misrepresent himself when necessary. This is not a clear and starry-eyed version of the American dream, not at all the Horatio Alger classic of a true-hearted young man who achieves enormous success through unceasing hard work and a moral compass that points true north.

In Gatsby we have both the good and the bad inherent in the American dream. The green light on the Buchanans' dock at which Gatsby stares so fixedly symbolizes money, of course, the ultimate fuel that powers the American dream. Tied closely to Gatsby's pursuit of that dream is another consistent character flaw: adultery and betrayal. In this harsh interpretation of the story, the seemingly honorable Nick Carraway is just another pimp arranging a sordid affair. Tom Buchanan's mistress, with all her awful airs, reflects the venality of adultery and the consequences that flow from it. Daisy and Jordan both have affairs, and Jordan is also a tennis cheat and a liar. Only Nick Carraway, who more or less floats above the fray, seems immune to the lure of that green light. At the novel's end the disillusioned young man decides to return home to the Midwest, America's heartland. The last words in the novel reflect the allure of the green light and how often those who pursue it will fail: "It eluded us then, but that's no matter—tomorrow we will run faster, stretch out our arms farther. . . . And then one fine morning—So we beat on, boats against the current, borne back ceaselessly into the past."

The leadership lessons from this fine novel are more subtle than in most of the other books on this list. When I look at the life of Jay Gatsby with the eyes of a leader, I think to myself, how could I have helped him? He clearly lacked a mentor, and his actual father appears only at his son's funeral. The lesson a leader ought to take from Gatsby the man is that sometimes our ambitions simply overwhelm us. We become so fixated on whatever version of the green light we are pursuing that we fail to see the damage our methods are causing.

I have encountered many subordinates and peers who had Gatsby-like instincts. The very difficult task is to harness the positive side of their ambitions—the willingness to work harder than anyone else, the bold (but not foolhardy) risk-taking, the innovation and creativity—while tamping down the darker urges. This has to be done with both honesty and subtlety, praising the good while curbing the bad. Jay Gatsby figures have been present in several of my commands at both high and low levels, and I have not always succeeded in finding the right balance in helping them reach for glory while avoiding the ill effects of doing so.

Part of my ambivalence about *The Great Gatsby* stems from the fundamental tragedy of Scott Fitzgerald's life. He achieved great success and fame as a young man in the early 1920s. Scott and Zelda were fixtures on the international social stage, from the Hemingway–Gertrude Stein–T. S. Eliot expat circle in Paris to the glittering nightclubs of New York at the height of the Roaring Twenties. In addition to his successful novels, he published dozens of well-regarded and popular short stories in the leading magazines of the time.

Despite its now-recognized brilliance, however, the novel's commercial struggles began Fitzgerald's inexorable slide into depression, alcoholism, and death. By the time he finished his final novel, *Tender Is the Night*, in the mid-1930s, he had decamped for Hollywood. Zelda meanwhile was dealing not only with alcoholism but also with severe mental illness that necessitated her admission to a mental hospital to treat schizophrenia (today we might diagnose her symptoms as bipolar disorder).

Fitzgerald failed to make it in Hollywood as a screenwriter (probably due at least in part to his untreated alcoholism). With Zelda institutionalized, he lived with another writer and attained sobriety toward the end of his life—but then suffered a heart attack and died in 1940, just before the United States entered World War II. Zelda outlived him by eight years, dying in 1948, troubled by mental illness to the conclusion of her life. Theirs is not a pretty and romantic story.

In the end, I decided to include the book here because it is so brilliantly written, and because its key message—that the American dream can be admirable and worth emulating—still resonates in our culture. But the undeniable warnings of *The Great Gatsby*—there is a dark side to success, a moral compass is crucial, and tragedy is always lurking somewhere ahead—are equally worth studying. I wouldn't send anyone into the world armed solely with a copy of the novel as a guide to living a fulfilling and happy life. But Gatsby's sheer ambition, his audacious reach for what he wanted, and his willingness to accept no artificial barrier to his success—ah, those qualities continue to appeal. Be careful how you reach for glory, it seems to me is the message, and be equally careful in the choices you make about what to reach for. Or put more simply, be careful what you wish for; the green light across the water may fool you into losing your way.

CHAPTER TWENTY-FIVE

UNDERSTAND THE HISTORY
The Guns of August
by Barbara Tuchman

> Nothing so comforts the military mind as the maxim of a great but dead general.

I have read many books of history over the years, as part of the curricula at Annapolis and various military war colleges and, above all, while doing my doctorate at the Fletcher School of Law and Diplomacy of Tufts University. Many were dense with facts and packed with unassailable truths; some were beautifully written, smooth, and readable. Of all the books of history I have read, however, the one that accomplishes both of these feats best is Barbara Tuchman's 1962 masterpiece, *The Guns of August*.

Beginning with its evocative title, a phrase that has been used again and again by statesmen and diplomats, generals and admirals, writers and commentators, the book simply grabs the reader by the throat and doesn't let go. Every time I pick up my battered first edition with plans to thumb through the first chapter or two, I find myself surrendering to the book's spell and realizing that I am going to read it cover-to-cover once again. And it's not as if I don't know how it is going to come out: the events of that fateful August will play out in bureaucratic folly, ego, and hatred. In four short years, the events outlined in the book led inexorably to the end of the Austro-Hungarian Empire, the end of the Ottoman Empire, and the end of the Russian Empire. The war that followed forever transformed the world's geopolitics.

Even more tragically, you can drop a plumb line from the opening chapter directly down to the unnecessary deaths of more than 20 million Europeans, roughly divided equally between civilians and military. Another 20 million at least were wounded, many of them grievously. It is no exaggeration to say that almost an entire generation of young European men was simply destroyed. The survivors were permanently affected by septic wounds, lungs damaged by mustard gas, and posttraumatic stress disorder (PTSD). They were, as Gertrude Stein said to Ernest Hemingway in the 1920s, "a lost generation."

One of the most important elements of leadership and indeed of life is understanding the *why* of events. This may be the most important aspect of the study of history, especially of the truly big tragedies. Without understanding why some cataclysmic event occurred, you are far more likely to repeat the mistakes and have the same terrible experience. As the old saw attributed to philosopher George Santayana in *The Life of Reason* goes, "Those who cannot remember the past are condemned to repeat it."

Thus, good leaders take the time not only to understand the facts of the historical record but also to appreciate the underlying causes. This is the difference between knowledge (necessary, but not sufficient) and wisdom. And this is true both in the big strategic questions (How did World War I start? Why was the United States unprepared for Pearl Harbor?) and in smaller, tactical situations (Why is my ship failing inspection after inspection? Why did I not recognize my team's bad morale sooner?).

In *The Guns of August* Tuchman seamlessly interweaves the historical record of those fateful first days of World War I with a reasoned and convincing analysis of how all those facts fit together into a coherent answer to the question of what caused this war. And, more important, what lessons we should learn that could permit us to back away from a similar situation in the future and perhaps avoid a similar catastrophe.

It is no coincidence that President John F. Kennedy and his brother Robert, along with other members of his inner cabinet, had this book in mind during the early days of the Cuban missile crisis—when a misstep could have meant hundreds of millions dead in a massive nuclear exchange. Kennedy specifically mentioned Tuchman's book on several occasions, alluding to his determination to avoid a similar tome being written about the ultimate ending of the Cuban crisis.

The book, which was awarded the Pulitzer Prize in 1963, opens with a startling and memorable image: the state funeral for King Edward VII of the United Kingdom, which was attended by no fewer than nine kings. One of them was Kaiser Wilhelm of Germany, the recently departed king's nephew. After laying out the scene in vivid detail, Tuchman concludes by saying, "on history's clock it was sunset, and the sun of the old world was setting in a dying blaze of splendor never to be seen again." It is an apt image of the lamps going out in Europe, not to be truly relit until after World War II. Indeed, Tuchman draws a straight line from the tragic events of August 1914 not only to the First World War, but to the Second as well.

One of the book's greatest strengths is its detailed attention to the war plans laid out by the great powers in the prewar period. Responding to the complex web of alliances set up by German chancellor Otto von Bismarck at the end of the 1870 war between France and Germany, both sides strove to lock in allies who would automatically come to their military aid and mobilize their forces in the event of a crisis. Of these plans, Tuchman gives pride of place to Germany's complex Schlieffen Plan and France's Plan XVII. Neither plan survived first contact with the enemy, but by laying them out in detail Tuchman provides a sound foundation for understanding the events that did unfold.

"The impetus of existing plans is always stronger than the impulse to change."

Plans are important to military people. The Pentagon, where I was assigned multiple times, and the NATO headquarters that I commanded in Belgium are both full of planners, although the vast majority of the plans they make will never be used. But as Gen. Dwight Eisenhower, the first Supreme Allied Commander of NATO, said, "the plan is nothing, but planning is everything," meaning that the more military teams come together to think through possible outcomes, the better. And my own corollary to that is the necessity of ensuring that military (and civilian) planning teams have access to the best historical data.

When I was the commander of U.S. Southern Command, I tasked our command historian and his team (who occupied a normally sleepy corner of the combatant command) to do "applied history." This meant that each month he was required to look around our vast area of responsibility—all the countries south of the United States in the Caribbean, Central America, and South

America—and find situations that needed historical explication to fully comprehend. You really can't understand Argentina today, for example, if you don't know the history of the Peronist Party. If you are going to be effective in Haiti, you need to understand how it gained independence and held onto it against all odds for decades while much of the rest of the region remained under colonial sway.

Barbara Tuchman's treatment of the outbreak of the war is the kind of history we need to return to again and again if we are to avoid needless war in the future. The heart of her work is the opening section on the assassination of Archduke Franz Ferdinand and his wife in Sarajevo by a Serbian revolutionary in late June 1914. She then outlines how the lethal flight of this single bullet touched off maneuvers in August that essentially left each of the major governments locked into mobilization and operations that—each believed—left them with no options but to prepare for and then march to war.

Tuchman then pivots to the execution of initial war plans on the two key fronts—the Western Front involving Germany, France, and the United Kingdom as the major military powers; and the Eastern Front, which involved mainly Russia and Germany. As a historian, she is careful to provide a balanced view that shifts the reader smoothly to and from the major capitals with profound visibility into Berlin, London, Paris, Moscow, and Vienna. She touches on the war at sea, which was just beginning to manifest as a significant factor in the conflict, presaging the importance of the unrestricted U-boat warfare that would ultimately drag the United States into the war. Tuchman also provides fascinating portraits of some of the key generals and political leaders, including Lord Kitchener of the United Kingdom; Helmuth von Moltke, leader of the German armed forces; King Albert I of Belgium; and General Joseph Joffre, the leader of the French armed forces.

By the end of *The Guns of August*, a careful reader is in equal parts satisfied with the detail inherent in this gripping tale of the start of a nearly apocalyptic war and mesmerized by Tuchman's ability to make scene after scene come to life. Her reflections on the inevitability that time would gradually grind down the morale of all the participants as casualties grew and the front lines remained relatively stagnant are vital to understanding the war in Ukraine more than a century later.

Her reoccurring theme is simple, if chilling: miscalculation, faulty communication, false narratives, and plain stupidity, coupled with almost willful obstinance, caused millions of deaths. In particular, she highlights the tactical incompetence and foolishness of various leaders (notably Kaiser Wilhelm); their failure to correctly assess the likelihood of a long and prolonged war given the relatively balanced capabilities of the protagonists; and their overreliance on the theory that nations that trade together (and are bound by blood ties among their royalty) are unlikely to end up in prolonged wars. All those assumptions proved not only false but deadly to millions of soldiers and civilians. In that regard, a companion book to Tuchman's is C. S. Forester's *The General*, a brilliant and tragic study of one fictitious leader in the war. Marine Corps general John Kelly, my close friend of decades, often recommends this novel to anyone headed for leadership of an organization. As a parable of deplorable leadership wrapped in the history of the bloody First World War it is hard to beat—and another example of leaders who use history to teach and explain the world to others.

I have always believed that good leaders are good readers, particularly of history, which provides the kind of intellectual capital that helps leaders make the best decisions no matter the field of endeavor. Knowing how past leaders have responded in crisis can provide powerful tools for those facing a crisis today.

Studying the Battle of the Atlantic in World War I, for example, helped American naval planners as they prepared to confront a resurgent German subsurface threat in World War II. History helped them immensely.

Additionally, reading history helps generate a necessary sense of proportion as we look at current challenges. When I led the NATO mission in Afghanistan, I would often pull open a volume of Churchill's memoirs of the Great War. Reading *The World Crisis, 1911–1918* helped to remind me that as hard as the fight in Afghanistan was on any given day, my military predecessors had faced casualties, failures, and sweeping dangers that dwarfed anything I was confronting. Perspective and balance are crucial for leaders, and understanding history is key to that.

Finally, by studying leaders who have faced immense challenges we learn about the attributes of leadership that can help us in the worst moments. I have several times read the powerful work of historical fiction about the battle of Thermopylae by Steven Pressfield, *Gates of Fire*. Pressfield's portrait of Leonidas, the Spartan king, who led his doomed three hundred Spartans to glory, death, and immortality against the Persian invaders is never far from my mind. In the face of overwhelmingly terrible odds, Leonidas was strong, brave, good-humored, realistic, and honorable. That is the sort of commander to have, regardless of the chances of victory or defeat. I am no Leonidas (although I am proudly Greek American), but the lessons I've learned by studying him have helped me be a better leader myself. Only by studying history, reading it deeply, and bringing it consciously forward into our own lives in the present day can we truly and deeply benefit from all that has gone before us.

So, I continue to pull Barbara Tuchman's superb work of history down from the shelf from time to time. It has never let me down in terms of giving me good ideas about command (and mistakes to avoid) and a sense of perspective as I face the day-to-day challenges of my life and career. Her brilliant narrative tale of a world consumed by fire as the result of failed leadership and human foibles is a fine example of the kind of book that allows current leaders to avoid tragic mistakes.

Understand the history. It makes all the difference.

CONCLUSION

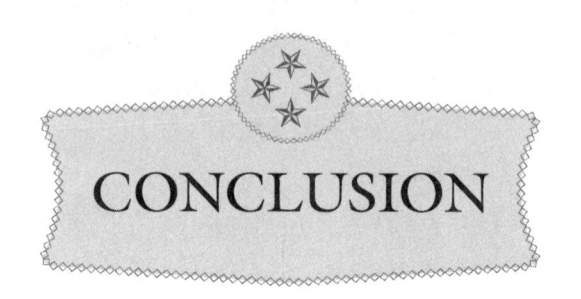

WHAT'S ON YOUR BOOKSHELF?

As I conclude this all-too-brief voyage through the very heart of my personal library of nearly five thousand books—including the twenty-five books presented here in *The Admiral's Bookshelf*—I find myself wanting to summarize why these particular books have meant so much to me, and more important, to help you, my readers, create your own bookshelf to help chart your course for life and leadership.

First, if you found this particular list of books compelling, excellent! I hope you will be inspired to pick up and read those with which you were not already acquainted, and to consider if they inspire you as they have me.

But second, and more importantly, I challenge you to assemble your *own* bookshelf. It is just a quick hop from the books I singled out to considering what *other* books have impacted the course of *your* life's voyage. Once you have assembled your list, I encourage you to distill a simple line or phrase from each that summarizes the wisdom the volume holds for you. That is the mission. Allow me to offer a brief methodology to approach this.

How can you build your personal bookshelf?

First, cast a wide net. Look at book reviews online, ask friends and coworkers for their recommendations, and peruse the shelves in your local bookstore.

Whether you end up with thirty books or a hundred, no matter. Now the hard part begins, which is quite simply culling the herd. Try to decide on the twenty or so volumes that have most deeply affected you and your life. When I began putting together *The Admiral's Bookshelf*, I started my search on the Internet and ended up with well over a hundred titles of acclaimed books. Then I walked through my home library and tried to match up the quality of the book and the meaning it had for me. But at this initial stage, the job is simply to generate a wide-ranging list of books.

You could organize your search according to the phases of your life, by the way. What books did you read in your teens that have stayed with you all these years? In addition to the brilliant *To Kill a Mockingbird*, which of course appears on my list, I can distinctly remember reading Ian Fleming's James Bond novels; diving into the science fiction of Isaac Asimov, notably the *Foundation* trilogy; devouring the three-volume fantasy epic *The Lord of the Rings*; and loving the adventure stories of Edgar Rice Burrows, from Tarzan to John Carter of Mars. Defining the works that shaped your worldview and personality as a very young man or woman can help you find the right initial set of books for your shelf.

In your twenties and thirties, as you were beginning or solidifying a career, you may have found your way to books ranging from the magisterial biographies of Walter Isaacson to the histories of Stephen Ambrose, David McCullough, and James McPherson, to the novels of Margaret Atwood and Ernest Hemingway. *The Sun Also Rises*, a book about friendship, betrayal, and, above all, about the pure enjoyment of life, had a profound impact on me as a twenty-something. Likewise, Atwood's brilliant early novels captured my hunger to understand the wide-ranging terrain of the human heart. Cormac McCarthy's lyrical, difficult, heartbreaking, and richly imagined *Blood Meridian* haunts me still.

In the prime of your career, as you sailed through your forties and fifties (for those of you who have gotten that far in life), perhaps you read books that captured the essence of your chosen profession. For me, of course, many of those were nautical classics, both fiction and nonfiction. I read my way through the works of Joseph Conrad and learned about command at sea by contemplating the mysteries of his brilliant novella *The Secret Sharer*. Historical fiction by C. S. Forester and Patrick O'Brian, notably the stories of sea captains Horatio Hornblower and Jack Aubrey, influenced my style of everything from leadership to ship handling. During times at sea I studied navigation and maritime operations and read the classics of my chosen way of life again and again, from Dutton to Crenshaw and many others. Each life path has its own rich literature, and plucking from that can help you assemble the right personal bookshelf for you. Many of these volumes, by the way, appear in an earlier book I wrote about the power of literature, *The Sailor's Bookshelf*.

And finally, you should focus on topics that speak to the passions of your life. I will admit that a wide range of subjects fascinate me. I could easily devote a lifetime, for example, to studying computer science and cyber security. Equally, I love the history of ancient Greece, from *The Peloponnesian Wars* to the *Anabasis* to the works of Steven Pressfield. Like many naval officers, I enjoy marine biology and ocean science. Yet another big part of my library—well over a hundred volumes—is devoted to the works and life of Winston Churchill. Those are my passions. The point is to know your own passions as subjects and make sure that your personal bookshelf has the right mix of volumes for you. Start by jotting down a few things that capture your imagination, be it fly-fishing, art history, antique cars, or whatever else might be important to you.

At this point you will have narrowed your scope to include the books that have fascinated you and fed your own passions. Now it is time to *really* cull the herd.

The best way to do this is to go down your list book by book, perhaps with a copy of the book in hand or on your computer monitor, and try to jot down a line or two of its wisdom. You are the best judge of how important the book is to you. Can you remember what it was about, name a couple of the characters or principals, and then extract a meaningful line or two of life or leadership guidance? If you can, the book is probably a keeper. If you are scratching your head and trying to come up with something in the book that matters, move on to the next book on your list.

Here I think brevity really is the key. If you can keep the summary short, crisp, and direct, you are on the right path. On the other hand, if you find yourself laboriously writing a lengthy paragraph to try and mine something meaningful, the book may not belong on the list.

At this stage, it is helpful to go through the selected book and pull out a few quotes that are distinctive and powerful. And don't hesitate, by the way, to use the power of a good search engine to find the "money lines" in the books. Searching for the best quotes in the novels of E. L. Doctorow, for example, can produce some fascinating ideas to expand your list. Winston Churchill is the most quotable man in history, perhaps just ahead of Hemingway. Harper Lee's slim volume *To Kill a Mockingbird* is full of powerful and memorable lines.

You have assembled a couple of dozen books by now, perhaps more, and for each of them you have distilled a line or two that captures the very heart of what the book has said to you. Now comes the final part, and in many ways the most important aspect of this exercise, which is tying this list of books and associated key thoughts to your life. Try to take the book and the associated thoughts (and quotes) and connect them to a moment in your own life—professional or personal—when what you learned from the book helped you navigate through a challenge, appreciate a wonderful moment, avoid a catastrophe, or put something into perspective.

For each of the books on your final bookshelf, you will want to have the book itself, some of the best quotations from it, your distilled wisdom, and an anecdote of how the book mattered for you. You may find that your bookshelf is larger than the twenty-five essential books on my shelf. Fifty books would not be a crazy number. Or, conversely, your personal bookshelf may be half a dozen volumes or even one powerful book that has surfaced again and again in your life. Perhaps the Bible or Dante's *Divine Comedy* or the *Odyssey* has provided everything you need to sail through life. Whatever the length of your bookshelf, it is the quality of what rests upon it that counts, and above all how those themes align with your own life and experiences. Mining the wisdom from my own bookshelf has helped me to see not only the power literature exerts on me, but also how meaningful certain moments in my own life, both personal and professional, have been. In the end, your life is a movie, a story that flows continuously through your given time in this world. But as I look back on my journey, there are a handful of still pictures, snapshots, that capture an important element or single moment.

By creating your own bookshelf, you give agency, voice, and life to those critical photographs, those crucial singular moments. You can turn those snapshots into a motion picture. And more important, you can attach them to given books and thus codify their importance. Your bookshelf is a wonderful way to review your own voyage, and perhaps to share it with friends and family, who will read the books on it, appreciate them, and draw upon them not only in their reading life but also in how they sail through their own portion of the vast sea we all sail.

I wish you Godspeed and open water as you decide what is on *your* bookshelf, and I sail on with the sincere hope that this old admiral's bookshelf is a help to you in the far more important task of assembling your own.

ABOUT THE AUTHOR

Adm. James Stavridis is a retired four-star naval officer who led the North Atlantic Treaty Organization in global operations from 2009 to 2013 as Supreme Allied Commander with responsibility for Afghanistan, Libya, the Balkans, Syria, counterpiracy, and cyber security. He served as commander of U.S. Southern Command, with responsibility for all military operations in Latin America from 2006 to 2009. Admiral Stavridis holds a Ph.D. in international relations and has published fifteen books and hundreds of articles in leading journals around the world. Admiral Stavridis is Chair Emeritus of the U.S. Naval Institute Board; Partner and Vice Chair, Global Affairs, at the Carlyle Group; and Chair of the Board of the Rockefeller Foundation. His most recent book is *The Restless Wave: A Novel of the United States Navy*.

The Naval Institute Press is the book-publishing arm of the U.S. Naval Institute, a private, nonprofit, membership society for sea service professionals and others who share an interest in naval and maritime affairs. Established in 1873 at the U.S. Naval Academy in Annapolis, Maryland, where its offices remain today, the Naval Institute has members worldwide.

Members of the Naval Institute support the education programs of the society and receive the influential monthly magazine *Proceedings* or the colorful bimonthly magazine *Naval History* and discounts on fine nautical prints and on ship and aircraft photos. They also have access to the transcripts of the Institute's Oral History Program and get discounted admission to any of the Institute-sponsored seminars offered around the country.

The Naval Institute's book-publishing program, begun in 1898 with basic guides to naval practices, has broadened its scope to include books of more general interest. Now the Naval Institute Press publishes about seventy titles each year, ranging from how-to books on boating and navigation to battle histories, biographies, ship and aircraft guides, and novels. Institute members receive significant discounts on the Press' more than eight hundred books in print.

Full-time students are eligible for special half-price membership rates. Life memberships are also available.

For more information about Naval Institute Press books that are currently available, visit www.usni.org/press/books. To learn about joining the U.S. Naval Institute, please write to:

Member Services
U.S. Naval Institute
291 Wood Road
Annapolis, MD 21402-5034
Telephone: (800) 233-8764
Fax: (410) 571-1703
Web address: www.usni.org